THE BLISS PAPERS

THE EXTRAORDINARY AWAKENING OF A HIGHLY SENSITIVE, ORDINARY WOMAN

B. ELIZABETH ATKINSON

For Amber and Justin who shine brightly
and kept me from the dark
And to Lily, our future

"What if you found out that the way spirit wanted to manifest through you was as a simple, ordinary person, but a person with great love, great compassion, and great wisdom? Maybe nobody would even recognize you. Nobody would acknowledge it in you, but it would simply be who and what you are. What if that was the way life wanted to manifest through you? Would that be okay with you? Would you allow that to happen?"

Adyashanti

Contents

It Begins

The earth was initiating me into the full flowering of my life. As I stood, it came with the force of a firehose, up through my feet. My eyes were closed and when the question formed in my silent mind, "What is this?" the answer followed clearly in one word: "Light."

This wave-like force had an electrical quality as it circulated my limbs, torso and head again and again in milliseconds; it came with a heat that caused me to immediately break out into beading sweat. Woozy and concerned about falling, I sat down as these energy waves pulled me into their sway.

Time passed and when the Light subsided, I grabbed a huge jug of water and gulped it down in one sitting. I was drenched in sweat, unclear about my experience. When it happened again, hours later during another still time, it claimed me. It seemed to have set off some kind of chain reaction within my body, an evolutionary biology in play, and put me on a course I could not have imagined. Thus, began my rebirth into wonder.

Introduction

In the late 90's, I had a major spiritual awakening as mentioned on the preceding page. It felt like a spontaneous rush of light running circularly through me (perhaps some kind of electro-magnetic waves). It began a physio, psychological, spiritual process that has changed my life in every way since it occurred. Prior to this, I poo-pooed anything new age. I wasn't a regular meditator nor did I have much background in spirituality, though I did soften to it a bit after watching Joseph Campbell's, *The Power of Myth* on PBS. I wouldn't hear of the Indian term, kundalini awakening, for another 2 years.

Although most spiritual traditions have a name for mystical awakenings, I call it a "Spontaneous Awakening of Light" (*SAL*) to keep it independent of any particular tradition and recognize that it was spontaneous (not sought after). What distinguishes a SAL is not the person who experiences it, but its nature as a spiritual encounter with an evolutionary biological process of consciousness.

Suffice to say, my perception of life changed, moving to an experience of the mystical and metaphoric. I eventually learned that the SAL experience culminates in an integration of the two poles of the psyche, leading to a sustained inner calm that resides in the present moment - the end of struggle (resistance), but not the end of learning.

An experience of light can happen anytime along a spiritual path. (For one example, see the Ken Burns film, *Seeing, Searching, Being - William Segal*, whose path began through painting.) Mine was well before any serious spiritual study; it was the SAL that initiated such study. Google was in its infancy and not much help at the time.

I began reading obsessively, book after book after book, trying to understand what this was all about. There was almost no one with whom I could speak about it in any depth, and that continued for many years, until three years later my daughter moved near me for her work. She became a witness to the changes and challenges that were occurring with the SAL and a student of it. Much later I realized how essential that witnessing was for me since I had no formal teacher. I was and am very grateful.

The early years of SAL were a time of psychic phenomena. Even with the examples of phenomena you'll see below (numbers 1–5), I was beset by doubt and felt awkward about the whole SAL experience.

1. Before the SAL, I was invited by a group of workmates on a lark to visit an intuitive. (She didn't like the term psychic.) I'd never done such a thing. I was told by the intuitive that I might have some kind of spiritual/psychic experience. As I went home and contemplated the possibility, I told myself that even though I had no idea what this was about and was a complete spiritual novice, I wanted whatever it was. I said "Yes, I want this," not knowing what "this" was nor the impact of that agreement. At the most, I thought I would "hear Gabriel" in the way this intuitive claimed she did; I didn't know anything else. (I was agnostic and thought I'd know more of God somehow.)

    The night after I said yes, I awoke for a few minutes to sense my entire body vibrating. My whole body seemed to be more alive with feeling; this happened several nights. Then one night I was awakened to feel movement coming up from my gut and, like a wave breaking on a beach, it carried information up to my head for my mind to interpret: an earthquake was going to occur. A few minutes later an earthquake hit the Bay Area where I was residing. It was the beginning of subtle psychic experience, just from consciously saying yes.

2. I decided to go to a Whole Life Expo on a whim, figuring people with experiences like mine might go to this. I thought the people might be a bit odd (which is how I felt about myself then) and was amazed to find hundreds of people from all walks of life.

There were booths of all types, a few pretty strange, some fascinating and some mundane. I came upon a booth that said Reiki for balancing energy. I'd been told to *balance my energy*, but I didn't know what that meant. I decided I should give this demonstration a try. (This was 20 years ago and I'd never heard about balancing energies or Reiki. It's a part of our vernacular now, but it wasn't then.)

I laid on a table, relaxed and closed my eyes, and a woman, Kathy, laid her hands on me. The first thing I noticed was that her hands were really hot. Skeptic that I was, I thought maybe she had put them on an electric hot pad or something. I finally realized this was silly.

Kathy coughed after a few minutes (this is important to the story later) and then told me I was going to be having interesting phenomena in my life (something like that, but more explicit). I wondered how she could know this.

She told me she was being told by the angels around me that I should sit on the ground with my legs apart a little (I later learned this had to do with grounding oneself), and that I needed to drink a lot more water.

She now had her hands slightly above my mid-section. A week or two prior to this, I had *wondered in my head* -- I'd said *nothing* to anyone -- about whether any experiences would be hampered by the fact that I had surgery done in the mid-section of my body. I now had some numbness there, some deadened nerve endings -- remember I didn't know anything about how these phenomena manifested.

Well, Kathy said, "Oh! This area is calloused. They are telling me to tell you that it doesn't matter; it won't make any difference." Now I was dumb-struck, absolutely dumb-struck!! I'd never met this woman in my life. She had no idea why she was telling me this, she just reported what she heard (or felt?). She went on to say a few more things and then said with tears, "Oh the angels are dancing around you. They want you to know if ever you are overwhelmed and disturbed by your experiences, just imagine them dancing around you."

I asked her if she was seeing this — her eyes were closed — and she answered with a wavering voice, "Apparently so," that my higher vibration was bringing up hers. When it was over, she explained that this had never happened to her before. Back to the cough I mentioned, she said she coughed because she was "hearing" this information but not speaking it out, and she was told that I needed to hear this information and if she didn't speak it out, it would get stuck in her throat (the source of her cough). Biologically, psychologically I find this very interesting.

By the way, what I wrote regarding Kathy was how *she* interpreted her experience with me; someone else might explain it differently. Even so, how this manifested is a mystery.

3. Kathy told me she could help "open me up quicker." She would make me a Reiki Master very quickly. I didn't know what all that meant then, but I said yes. (And I did find the initiation odd, didn't know why it would do anything, but I was open to all this newness which proved to be a good thing.)

Kathy and I became friends and she worked on me energetically a number of times and taught me some things. One of those times, I came in and hopped on the massage table. During the first year after the SAL, I could track energy. When her hand touched me, I would feel the energy zipping around to its destination.

So, there I was feeling great and Kathy began her Reiki treatment. I said, "Oh, I'm feeling it come up..." and then my neck jutted backwards involuntary and I couldn't speak well. I managed to get out, "It feels like something has come up my body into my throat." "You mean like a stake," she asked? The minute she said that I burst into tremendous sobs. At that same time, all of a sudden, "I," my consciousness, was out of my body and over somewhere to the left of head. I knew my body was sobbing, but "I" didn't feel it at all. *I* felt fine.

In the stillness, a voice not unlike my own said, "This body just needs to do this." I wasn't floating over my body like a near–death experience. I "saw" nothing, heard nothing but that voice. I just knew that what I thought of as me was not in my body.

When it was over, I was back in my physical body without any fanfare. Simple as that. I felt no trauma, no residue of emotion. Nothing. Poor Kathy was crying with empathy, not knowing I had felt no emotional pain or sadness during this experience.

4. About a month or less after the SAL, I noticed that when I went to bed and inadvertently had my hands on my body, I felt these energy sensations going up and down my whole body. It was disconcerting and hard to fall asleep, so I began sleeping without my hands on my body in any way. I also started having unusual body jerks now and then. The first place these jerks occurred was in my legs; later they moved to other places. (In the Indian kundalini experience there is a name for these body movements; although mine were a bit different, I learned they went with the experience of a SAL.)

    This light or energy was now *always present*. I didn't have to do anything; it was just there. It's part of me still. Feeling energy in my body is second nature to me now, though I don't track it anymore. It's not separate from me. You'll know what I mean by this when you read *The Nature of Bliss* paper.

5. Also, in those early years, I saw pictures in my third eye - that inner place that can be found between your eyebrows when your eyes are closed and you look slightly upward. Here's how they went: as I was preparing to sleep, once I

closed my eyes, I noticed that in my third eye a white screen, of sorts, came across the aperture and an animated picture appeared. The entire episode was accompanied by a deeply relaxing state that came over me.

The first picture I ever saw was of a buffalo roaming the plains. I had no control over when these scenes came or what played out. The aperture closed down and soon I drifted off to sleep. Later, one "vision" at a time, I saw a steam locomotive, then a hot-air balloon and then an airplane. It was like a history of advancement into the West. Later I would see more random things. Once, I saw myself, in video form, walking on the city sidewalk with a woman not far behind me, almost like she was accompanying me.

A few years into these experiences, my vision expanded in this way: I was laying on my bed relaxing with my eyes closed mid-day. I saw a black man all dressed in white. Somehow, I knew that he was from one of the islands that England had colonized long ago. Because of that, I assumed if he spoke, he'd have a British accent.

As I was watching, the aperture slowly expanded, bigger and bigger, until there were no borders, and I was lying on my bed with this man at the foot of it. He never spoke, but when I saw this, I gasped in fear and the vision shut down immediately. What was that? Might these "visions" come from the same place as the images that make up our dreams? Was the man a waking dream of some kind? A spirit? I have questions, not answers.

I loved having these pictures, but over a few years, I noticed that they didn't seem to serve any great purpose. Like all the phenomena, it did show me there is much more to life and our biology than we know. I realized I needed to let go of any attachment I had to the pleasure of these phenomena and continue to grow in consciousness toward the peace of All There Is.

Then about one-and-a-half years into this process of integration, I found myself periodically having an intuitive need to put pen to paper. I did not come up with a particular issue and will myself to write about it. Instead, the subject showed itself via some confusion with which I was struggling, often unconsciously. Then essays with answers came effortlessly bringing with them wisdom, understanding and resolution that was often symbolic and certainly calming to me.

I had been raised Catholic as had generations of my ancestors before me. Although this is certainly not the case for all Catholics nor necessarily inherent in its teachings, Catholicism was taught to me in a very fear-based manner and with a literal interpretation that made no sense to me.

Not understanding the ramifications, my mother used her faith to discipline me: "God's going to punish you for that." Or, when I looked in the mirror as a little girl, "The devil's going to jump out and get you!" These and other such daily pronouncements solidified God as a negative and harsh disciplinarian. "He" was a separate entity living apart from me. His retribution became something to fear, and, for me, there was no love to be found.

Unfortunately, at the time, catechism and all but a handful of clergy I encountered, served only to strengthen this fear. Not surprisingly, I didn't like church or catechism and left it the minute I was living on my own. Nevertheless, I was thoroughly indoctrinated; the fears and apprehensions I associated with God and Catholicism lived deep in my psyche.

Many of you may have had similar, unfortunate experiences with your own upbringing in religion or simply your acquaintance with it. By the time my awakening occurred, I had turned off to the idea of God, and couldn't even use the word God because of what it conjured up: the judgmental, bearded old man.

Nevertheless, I had to make sense out of what had happened to me in this experience of Light, and I continued reading intensely for a number of years. What I learned was certainly different from the fear-based teachings of my youth. As I read "new thought" literature and books from other spiritual paths, a lot of it made sense to me, especially when utilizing metaphor, Eastern or Native American beliefs and integrating science. I am forever indebted to those authors and deeply grateful for their insights and teachings. These readings helped me since I found some aspects of new age talk ungrounded - free-floating without a rooted system.

I wasn't aware that someplace deep within me conflict existed between these new ideas I was reading and adopting and my past indoctrination. Internally, I must have longed for it all to make some kind of rational sense.

It was when I began writing the first two papers that I realized my psyche was formulating this "rational sense": a way for me to metaphorically reinterpret my Catholic past and marry it to all I had recently read and learned.

(Oh, and once I'd quieted down this internal struggle with the early indoctrination of my mind, I didn't run back to Catholicism or any religion. What I wrote in these next papers was a way for me to continue on *my* path without that 18 years of dogma chasing me and messing with my mind.)

Eventually, as more and more inspired papers came, I realized I was writing things essential to *my* personal understanding of Spirit: an adjunct, of sorts, to any path I read about in books. These papers came to me as stand-alone essays with several months or more between them, so some themes may be repeated. They were deeply intuitive, and spontaneously written. They are somewhat poetic in quality.

The Bliss Paper essays, noted by a spiral, became a way for me to open my heart fully to Life. I don't present them as *Truth*, but rather a metaphoric interpretation by which Truth could blossom fully *within me.* The first two of these essays that came to me are related to Catholic Christianity (*An Integration of East and West*, and *Five Stages Inherent in an Awakening*). This needn't stop you from gaining meaning from them if your own religious teachings were different or non-existent.

I am sharing these writings because they may speak to you - in part or as a whole - and help you with your own disparity of thought about the spiritual nature of life and the *state of love* that encompasses it all.

The Explorer

Watching Africa on television,
The wide-open plains once unknown,
I wonder about the adventurous life,
And me sticking so close to home.

There is a romance to wandering,
And I am captive to its call.
But the voice I feel comes from within,
Echoing vast expanses and disintegrating walls.

I am an explorer of creative places,
Of spaces still unseen.
I feel things I've never felt before,
Hear songs I've yet to sing.

This inner safari is limitless,
Harbors the discerning, spiritual eye.
Full of courage and loving wisdom,
It discovers a world that never dies.

B. Elizabeth Atkinson

The First Year

The first year of the SAL was a bit like a honeymoon. Excited by my experience and their own budding spirituality, a friend of mine and her daughter-in-law and my daughter and I would meet most weeks to experiment with healing energy. I was the "tracker" and could tell them, when they put their hands on me, where the energy was going. They all had their own way of experiencing things.

I experimented with other modalities also and joined a few healing volunteer groups, one for AIDS. I learned a great deal during this time, my body often the teacher. I was very, very open and shouldn't have been doing healing at all. What did I know! I was fearless. A few times at the AIDS building, I'd be working on someone and literally be throw back against the wall. What was that about!

I thought everything was new and wonderous. If I put my hand on any number of objects, such as a rock or a spoon, I felt its vibratory energy. I'd go around touching everything because it all seemed so magical. Yet from the get-go, I pondered the biology of it all: how did this light episode happen; what causes the phenomena to play out in my body; what had been triggered in my body to allow all this? I still wonder.

I didn't traditionally meditate before the SAL. Now I laid down and was still, my closed eyes going toward the inner third eye area. I usually saw purple or lavender, sometimes a bit of white and gold. Laying there, my body felt like it moved magnetically deeper into the bed towards the earth. (That movement doesn't occur much anymore.)

In that still time, I would sometimes have what I came to call "releases." This because I'd cry (of sorts). I didn't know about what and it was often without tears, just noise. I look back now and wonder if it was both my body's own release of whatever and also things I had empathically picked up. I wasn't sad; I just let it happen.

Nevertheless, that first year was joyous. I had amazing dreams that were often archetypal. For instance, I was Arthur pulling the sword from the stone or Helen of Troy came down from Mt. Olympus. I was seeing things in my third eye that I mentioned. I was childlike in my wonder and curiosity. I could hardly believe all these new experiences or that I could touch someone and they'd feel heat or movement. What was this?!

At the end of that first year, I moved and remember a time when I was sitting on the floor of my new bedroom, paper strewn around and a pen nearby. I was a bit crazed. A lot of information was being "downloaded" into my mind with great speed. I was grabbing for paper and pen to get it all down, but it was impossible. I do remember a theme about this experience of SAL being evolutionary or we were in an evolutionary time. I wish I could be more specific for you, but I got little more from this download on a conscious level.

I'm sure anyone seeing me on the floor during this process would have found it disconcerting. When I later looked at whatever snatch of words I got down on paper, it wasn't worth saving. (By the way, I borrowed the descriptive computer word, *downloaded,* from Adyashanti who used it to describe an experience he had similar to mine. I read his book, <u>The End of Your World</u>, during the latter years of my process and found it comforting and affirming.)

So many experiences were occurring this year and the next several years! I didn't know the term kundalini yet, which would eventually help me understand my SAL experience. Oddly enough, a postcard advertisement came to me out of the blue touting a rerelease of Gopi Krishna's, <u>Kundalini, the Evolutionary Awakening Energy in Man</u>. The side-bar spoke about certain symptoms that were familiar.

I immediately ordered the book. Sure enough, there were enough similarities between Gopi Krishna's experience and my own, that I realized this was the light experience that I had had. Unlike his and other Indian guru's writing of kundalini, I didn't think the light was coiled at the bottom of the chakra's. My experience was that it came up from the earth through my feet and circulated. Nevertheless, I had found the name associated with my experience. I renamed it what it was for me, a *Spontaneous Awakening of Light* - a SAL.

All this newness and reading! I needed a path. My intuitive writing started about a year-and-a-half after this honeymoon first year.

I've placed the "Pick a Path" paper next, near the beginning of these essays, even though it wasn't an initial writing. It sets the tone for *The Bliss Papers*, but came in stages over a few years.

Pick a Path

" ...metaphor is the basis of all language and thought, as it is of all religion." Thomas Cahill, The Gift of the Jews

"Myth is the...indispensable intermediate stage between unconscious and conscious cognition." Jung

"All descriptions of reality are temporary hypothesis." Buddha

A Native American Ojibway elder once told me, "Pick a path; pick a path; you've got to pick a path." At the time, I did not understand the importance of a path and the power of ritual. There are a variety of paths from which one can choose to arrive at the destination for which we are all bound. Most are grounded, and well-worn - etched in the collective psyche that honors and builds on what came before. Some, like mine, came individualized from within.

Yet before this choice occurs in earnest, many of us must heal our past acquaintance with religion and the specific inculcation of it in our childhood. I came to see this in my own experience of spiritual awakening. Raised in Catholicism, I never fully embraced it, but its impact reverberated for years. As much as I wanted to ignore it, it was a deeply entrenched part of me. I tried to put it out of my mind. To me the feminine was barely visible and Jesus had been co-opted, the seeming poster-boy for the religious right. (Blasphemous, I know.)

After I experienced a spontaneous awakening of light (SAL) rushing up my body and all its ramifications, I began experiencing a variety of psychic phenomena as mentioned. Not the least of which was a vision of Christ ascending/resurrecting, angels all around, except *I* was Christ. It was Christ, and I was Christ. We were one in the same.

I was startled and taken aback. I was raised that this was blasphemy (once again that word) and, having rejected Christianity and uncomfortable with even the word *God* at the time, I was mystified to be witnessing such a sight. I had no place in my mind to interpret this scene and was not ready to embrace it, so I ignored it. Several years later I realized that this "ascension into heaven" was a metaphor for transcending ego through the Christos (integration), the one with which my psyche was familiar.

What I realized over several years was that the energy coursing through me after my awakening needed a path – a route undeterred by my ego-self's fears and misperceptions. This is what the stories and beliefs of major religions and indigenous peoples are all about; *without such a path, havoc can ensue.*

Our thoughts and beliefs give form to light and shadow, then rituals concretize them. These thoughts and beliefs are so powerful, so instrumental in creating our lives, that without a conscious path, our clouded unconscious can have free reign. This unconscious is also connected with cultural and human archetypes, both positive and negative, and with the collective unconscious.

To the extent we are "in the dark" about our inner motivations, our hurts, biases, judgments and resentments, to that extent will we sabotage our intentions and desires and get in real psychic trouble on the mystical journey.

When I encountered spiritual phenomena, I needed a contextual roadmap for these experiences of the unknown, one that could take me from here to there. (Hence the Bliss Papers.) Belief or spiritual systems provide this, as do their various practices.

Jesus, Buddha, Mohamed, Mary and other masters of world religions transcended ego consciousness to become the Christos, the Light that forges a bridge to the Divine as described by sages and mystics. Their teachings show us the way. So too the spirit and animal guides and totems within the belief systems of indigenous people.

Also, at the time of my experience, it felt to me as though some energy field boundaries were dissolved with this SAL. Although difficult times are a cleansing part of any deep, experiential spiritual path, I think things may have been easier for me had I been involved with a particular system and had a teacher to guide me.

It would have helped also if I'd known about my highly sensitive, empathic nature, but that research hadn't been done yet. Nevertheless, there is an inner guidance that comes with a SAL. I was guided to books and authors that helped me immensely. I was protected from any kind of breakdown and my personal path was coming to me via the inspired Bliss Paper essays.

One example of a need for a path came shortly after my SAL. It was suggested early on that I "lay hands" on others, and I was open to it. It was a time when a lot of Reiki and healing modalities were becoming popular. Although I never had an advertised healing practice and worked mostly on a few friends or their friends, when I did so, I began to feel and physically express the person's emotion and its symptomatic cause.

For instance, when I put my hands on a healthy-looking woman I didn't know (a friend of a friend), all of a sudden, I was having trouble breathing. I sputtered out a question as to whether she had some kind of problem going on. She said she didn't, but after I kept gasping for air she said, "Well I do have asthma." The minute she said that, my breathing difficulty stopped. I later learned that this was because she "owned" it; it wasn't mine. It was a number of years before I understood that this was an empathic ability (or a liability at the time, since my energetic boundaries were still far too open).

These experiences often left me confused and overwhelmed. Over time, my misplaced sense of responsibility was depleting me, and I became physically and emotionally exhausted. I was being shown the depth of my empathic abilities long before I even knew the term. This was an example of a physio-spiritual manifestation of what can occur when the authentic power of the feminine is repressed personally and culturally, and we meet other's needs at the expense of our own.

Although all this was part of my clearing and education process, a rooted path and teacher may have moved me through it quicker, mitigating some of these problems and addressing some of my distorted ideas. I needed my own personal spiritual path, one that came from interpreting what I experienced and sensed within.

During this time, I began to recognize my own inner blocks. For example, I saw I had a knee-jerk reaction to Jesus and my Catholic upbringing that needed to be healed. Fear and judgment would only hamper the awakening process and had to be addressed.

I began this healing by simply acknowledging the need for it. I studied and learned much from Native American, Buddhist, Hindi, Judaic, Tao, new thought and other paths. This also helped me to accept and appreciate that all major religions hold similar core beliefs, that many of their stories are metaphor based on historical reality, and that they seem to have evolved over thousands of years from past belief systems. It was the intolerance of dogma, patriarchy and literal interpretation that didn't suit me.

A year later, unplanned and while reading a novel, I felt an inspired urge to put pen to paper and, to my surprise, out came the first of these essays--a simple interpretation of the Christ story that combined east and west and brought in the Divine Feminine. It was as if I'd pushed a button and initiated a computer program in my mind that wove together the religious input of my youth and the spiritual awareness I had gained from my recent readings to formulate an outcome acceptable to my psyche.

And so it was. It brought a deep peace to a difficult struggle of belief that was just below the surface, unknown to me. Though I have never returned to any formal religion, it taught me that I needed to acknowledge the spiritual heritage that went back for generations in my family and integrate it in all I'd learned.

Now I identify the essence of God with the light of consciousness; I found a metaphoric way of expressing this experience of the Divine in the 21st century. As Peter Russell notes in his book, *From Science to God*, "For spiritual development to be acceptable, it must be reasonable. It must make sense within the current world view...a reformation of the timeless wisdom in a contemporary context."

And so these papers and poems continued spontaneously, one after the other over a few years, until the last one when I realized I had written a personal path for myself and answered questions pertinent to me. Life became a mystical journey, experiential and experimental.

Whether we retain the faith of our childhood, reinterpret it as I did mine or choose a different path altogether, *it behooves us to heal any negative effects of the religion in which we were raised, learn to honor its truth, as well as the truth which exists in all the major teachings* - from Goddess traditions, indigenous peoples, the major world religions and new thought.

In addition, because the Judeo-Christian tradition is woven deeply into the very fabric of our culture and its archetypes, each of us - *regardless of belief* - must find a peace of our own making with it. We may have ignored it and thought it no longer affected us. Usually it still does.

Many of us don't give up struggle and become an integrated whole without healing negative issues we may have either with our religious upbringing or our Christian culture. Then we must choose (or return to) a grounded path that provides a bed on which the Great Mystery may rest, a roadmap that gives form to the Light that wishes to be acknowledged in each of us.

The first of what I would eventually call, The Bliss Papers, intuitively came to me one morning, maybe a year-and-a-half or more into the SAL. I may have been thinking about religion and the way I was raised, but I don't remember. I always kept paper and pencil beside my bed because I'd wake up with interesting dreams and wanted to quickly write them down (and return to sleep if it was in the middle of the night).

This wasn't a dream. As I put pen to paper and began to write, the meaning became clear. It was an attempt to bridge my unconscious discrepancies between some new thought teachings and those of my Catholic indoctrination. In the end, all the Bliss Papers would be about inner discrepancies - difficulties of understanding about what I read or heard and what I thought-- struggles that needed resolution.

During the first five or so years after the SAL, I had a lot to heal around my Catholic indoctrination. For instance, I might intellectually understand that God (All There Is) wasn't outside of me, a bearded old man that judged me. Yet I hadn't embodied that idea at all. Even after writing these papers, it took a long time for me to fully experience and embrace their contents.

I'm sure, like me, that many of you on your own journey read or hear things that make sense to you, but they don't become a part of you. That usually takes some "aha experiences" that slowly grow it inside you.

A few weeks or more after the first paper, another one came that was associated with it. It would seem I was still looking for ways to interweave my Catholicism with the awakening journey. Remember, they pertain to me and you may or may not relate to them.

Here is that first paper followed by the second one.

New Thought Christianity:
A Metaphor for Integration of East and West

FYI: Yin/Shakti/Mother Earth is feminine: the wisdom-filled, dynamic, mysterious stillness that holds the ground of everything and appears passive. Yang/Shiva/Father Sky is masculine: the dynamic, active, outward expression of this inherent creativity. Society has interpreted these feminine/masculine traits literally as gender, and this misinterpretation gave rise to the idea that women were passive supporters of men, who were the "doers" — patriarchy and inequality followed. In truth, we are each made up of the authentic power of yin and yang, feminine and masculine, the two poles of the psyche, and when these are balanced, wholeness can be achieved.

All Life is balance. Mary (symbolizing yin/right brain) is the incubation, birthing and nurturing of all creativity. Jesus (symbolizing yang/left brain) is the outward dynamic expression of that creativity. There *cannot* be one without the other. There is circular movement between the two visualized as the infinity symbol.

This world consists of the constant jockeying and tension of duality, i.e., good/bad; right/wrong; male/female; heaven/earth. Yet Divine Love is the absence of conflict; there is nothing that is not "of Spirit," so there is an inner desire for the peace of unity. That desire is fulfilled when all elements of yin and yang balance and coalesce through love and acceptance of our selves and each moment as it is. This is an all–encompassing act of forgiveness. It includes forgiving ourselves, others and the suffering inherent in duality. We say "Yes!" and embrace *what is;* that embrace is the mortar of integration facilitated by the unifying Spirit of Holy Wisdom (known as Sophia and often called the Holy Spirit).

It was no accident of storyline that Mary (yin) was at the foot of the cross. Jesus (yang) died completely to the Divine (represented by the center-point, the zenith of the four directions of the cross), meaning he transformed via surrender of ego-self and transcended duality by uniting masculine and feminine and becoming a catalyst for the Holy Spirit (Holy Wisdom).

Jesus as *redeemer* is Christ energy that transforms our suffering by liberating us from ego-bound captivity that assists us in resurrecting our long repressed feminine. Struggle ends: the ego and its experience of separation surrenders the lead to our Divine Nature, our non-dual Self. This opens the door to personal transformation that alters our perceptions and brings us the inner peace of being at one with All That Is (non-duality).

As with all religious stories, the Christian one is based on historical knowledge. It provides metaphors and an archetype for our psyche: a path for transformation. (In Christianity, for instance, Jesus *dying for our sins* means he paved the way for direct access to personal transformation with an evolved consciousness.) From this viewpoint, three elements stand out as different from literal Christianity:

1) Rather than focusing on the *sacrifice* of Jesus on the cross, often leading to the self as worthless sinner, the focus is on the resurrection of Self as a joyous expression of Divinity;

2) Rather than negating the joys of the earthly or physical, the focus is on heaven *and* earth as a dynamic of balance—the practical, the scientific, the Earth herself, as part of the holy and ethereal;

3) Rather than focus on any one aspect of the Trinity, the focus is on the *dynamics of transformation,* the integration of the feminine, masculine and Holy Wisdom.

Through transformation of ego-self, the masculine unites with the feminine igniting the third aspect, the light of the Holy Spirit. That ignited Spirit of Holy Wisdom sparks us, fills us with light, and guides us through the pitfalls of our misperceptions to our Divine Nature, slowly triggering a sustained inner peace as we live in the moment with All There Is (transfiguration). Here we join the masculine and feminine of the transformed Son and with the ignited Spirit, add to the evolution of consciousness and become a conduit of Love active in the world.

The incredible gift we share is our power to choose. Yet, *ultimately, there is only one choice from which all else flows:* Each of us stands in the Ground of All Being. Our purpose is to awaken to this truth and, with the power of forgiveness and redemptive grace, allow our inner transformation to unfold: our individual, spontaneous, creative expression undifferentiated from All There Is.

Five Stages Inherent in a Sustained Awakening

Metaphorically Relating Christianity to the Native American 7-Directions, Eastern Thought, and the Birthing Process

1) **The Annunciation; Mother Earth and Father Sky; The Agreement:** As with Mary, an agreement that is made deep in the soul to conceive the Light, to "know" God. When this is sincerely echoed in our own life, it sets the stage for the integration of masculine and feminine: Mother Earth and Father Sky; Yin and Yang; Shakti and Shiva, etc.

2) **Immaculate Conception; South, Snake, Innocence; Spiritual Conception:** Initiating the process of integration, light infuses our body, as it did in Mary's immaculate conception, Jesus's baptism, through a master's touch, or with any awakening of light. (FYI: this stage could be anywhere along the path.)

3) **Lent; West, Jaguar, Introspection; Gestation:** Growth within occurs psychically, emotionally, physically and spiritually; for a while, digestion can be affected. Just as with pregnancy, we have little control over the process. Our job is to notice the

signs within and learn from the growth that occurs. During this time, difficult learning and clearing are often interlaced with joy, insights, psychic phenomena and the need to be alone in nature. Our will slowly yields to the Divine as we move toward the still point between the two opposite poles of the psyche. This is the unitive stage.

4) **Good Friday; North, Buffalo, Wisdom; Labor:** As if testing our spiritual unity with God, feelings of abandonment, despair and powerlessness arise – dark nights. We recognize and feel more deeply our resistance, humbly bringing us to Divine Paradox and essential wisdom. By *allowing* (surrendering), we receive the grace to accept what is, forgive and receive the endless love of the Universe. A tipping point is reached; Jesus as redeeming light is free to transform ego–self and release it from the captivity of resistance.

5) **Easter; East, Eagle, Illumination; (Re)Birth:** *With the integration of the two poles of the psyche, masculine and feminine,* the earth and sky energies, Self can be resurrected, triggering a sustained *state of love.* That state of love is the experience of non–separation, characterized by continued growth (*without* struggle) and spontaneous wisdom as we live in the present moment, take our rightful part in Divinity with Jesus and become a manifestation of Holy Spirit. No longer you *and* God; you *are one* with God; that is, we are not separated from All That Is. (This separation was perception, not Truth.) We may begin the path of resurrection praying *to* All There Is, but we end by *blessing* All There Is — *our life becomes the prayer.*

We human beings just lump together everything in the universe which is beyond the capacity of all of us, and to all those things together some of us give the name God. ...There is a creative force beyond us. ...There is a sustaining power that keeps planets in their orbit. ... There is something motivating towards constant change in the universe. ...God is a creative force, a motivating power, an overall intelligence, and ever- present, all pervading spirit which binds everything in the universe together and gives life to everything. ...I could not be where God is not. You are within God. God is within you.

Peace Pilgrim

Purpose and Passion

There is only one purpose and it is the same for everyone: to become conscious by fully loving and accepting ourselves. Let me repeat this: *our only purpose is to become conscious.* Everything else flows from that; all service flows from that. This doesn't mean we might not be volunteering and working for issues and organizations we care about while we're becoming consciousness; it means we can stop knocking our head against the wall when some of the spiritual literature and teachers are telling us to find our purpose.

All the relationships, issues, good and ill fortune that we encounter within the scope of our life are those we attract, and they provide us with opportunities for growth. This growth to bring more of our unconsciousness to light often comes through struggle with what is, but as we become more and more conscious, the need for learning through struggle ends; we simply notice. Consciousness also requires taking time for silent reflection, contemplation and/or some type of meditation; any number of books and workshops exist to help us incorporate this into our busy life.

Our *passion*, on the other hand, *is our individual creative expression of that which moves us and to which we commit with integrity.* It includes creative work in literature, music, home skills, cooking, drama, helping the poor and deprived, research, teaching, works of art and architecture, commerce, equality and social justice, healing, science and math, increasing environmental awareness and any number of other great endeavors. Our passion is an avenue through which we can become conscious, and when fueled by our purpose, it contributes to the conscious evolution of our species and the world.

It is our passion on which we may be unclear, not our purpose. Some people have found their passion in the current work they do; unfortunately, they are in the minority. For most of us, our daily job may be less than satisfying. Nevertheless, our reactions to it can provide us with opportunities to grow in consciousness. Let everything serve your purpose and eventually your passion will show itself. As our consciousness becomes more and more clear, we become clear on what meets our needs and what we're passionate about. It's a paradox that the more conscious we become through forgiveness, acceptance, self-love and meeting our own needs, the more our needs will serve others. We don't need to figure it out; simply put, we're called to acknowledge our divinity within by growing in consciousness and staying alert to its signs in our lives and in our bodies. All else falls into place over time and becomes effortless. *As we embrace our purpose, our passion shows itself.*

Our commitment to consciousness and our own creative passion assist the evolution of consciousness in all people. Who we are and all we bring to this world are more valuable than we realize.

B. Elizabeth Atkinson

The whole world is a series of miracles...but we're so used to them, we call them ordinary things.

Hans Christian Anderson

I began wondering about the bliss I was reading about. Some Indian guru's spoke of it and it sounded like this other-worldly, ethereal state. Joseph Campbell famously referred to it – "Follow your bliss." Other than the pure euphoria I felt for a few days after the SAL, which you could call Bliss, I didn't really get it. I was having a lot of phenomena occur during these years, but nothing I'd call Bliss. Maybe it's a definition thing.

I was also noticing that I didn't track or experience energy within me in quite the same way. (You'll understand what I mean when you read the paper below.) So once again, I found myself writing what I felt about this conundrum. This feeling of words allowed me to come up with intuitive answers, and I wrote like this again and again in future papers.

The Nature of Bliss

"One must be utterly abandoned to God... otherwise all is folly and meaninglessness." Carl Jung

"There are two ways to lead your life. One is as though nothing is a miracle. The other is as though everything is a miracle." Albert Einstein

Think of a winter day when you are very cold. You decide to draw a nice warm bath that is just right and when you get in that perfectly warm bath you find yourself bathed in joy. You ooh and aah with glee as you begin to warm up. The coldness ekes out of you, dislodged by the warmth.

Imagine this as being bathed in Light as you come into balance with *All That Is* and realize this Light is within you and all around you. Your comfort level is sustained by Spirit—not too hot and not too cold. And what at first was a peak experience of oohs and aahs as your body adjusted to the water may seem temperate now because you are no longer dazzled by it; *there is no longer a division between what you experienced as warmth and the warmth itself.* You are not separate from it.

Now extend this metaphor to a bath of Light without the boundaries of a tub; everything that exists is in the bath with you, and everything, including you, *is* this bath of Light-the Light of Divine Love expressing itself in form. (This is not just intellectually understood; it is experienced.)

This is the Bliss that is talked about in some spiritual literature. It is not the high emotional state with which we often associate it. You can't will this state into being;

it comes with grace. You experience a kinship of Spirit with all that is and no longer identify with duality. Resistance and separateness fall away as Love slowly envelops you and lives through you.

Though you still grow and learn, you do so *without* struggle. Unshakeable in all things, you "flow with the river" and its current carries you. Like passing clouds, some thoughts and emotions still come, but they move on as you do not attach to them. Simply put, you are a *witness* to the passing parade *at the same time as you exist and create within it.* This sustained state of awakening brings contentment and calm joy.

We don't become still to *find* God; we are still to become *aware of God manifest within us.*

There are those of us who try to avoid knowing our true *Self;* we are afraid of what we'll find. Deeply judging ourselves and others, we avoid the responsibility and acknowledgment of our discontent through a *constant* distraction of television, clutter, chatter and the like that robs us of ourselves as we invest our energy and emotions in the other. By this avoidance we shortchange our opportunity to invite balance into our lives and know our own Divinity.

Then there are those of us who become attached to the peaks, the oohs and aahs when we first put our "cold body in the nice warm bath," and grab onto that "high" as bliss, mistaking excitement for joy. We are afraid to let go, trust, and allow true, *sustained* Bliss (calming Love) to bubble-up *from within.* We seek to recreate another peak experience, and use our will and energy to try and "make it happen." It can even become some kind of addiction, like sex, food, the perfect body/image, money, possessions, work, gambling, alcohol, endless spiritual workshops and experiences, drugs and so on.

Because these emotional peaks are necessarily short-lived, we rush here and there to find more, creating instead a good deal of struggle for ourselves. Attached to the highs, we may assume the peaceful state described above is boring, blah, a flat-line experience. But this is not so.

Bliss is a state of love (not emotional love), the experience of kinship with *All That Is*, the culmination of the rebirth of the non-dual *Self*, and is without those high peaks (and their ever-present partner, valleys). Yet it's full of wisdom and love, so deep, it is ever vibrant.

Glowing with a pervasive sense of well-being, it does not participate in past reflection and regret or in the anxiety of what the future may bring. It lives in the moment—in the glistening vibrancy of Love that is nature, is each person and is everything—and is full of Beauty and the boundless wisdom that exists in the Now. It feels ordinary and openly accepts the sacredness present in all Life, including our own. In this calm state of sustained Bliss, our life is the prayer and blesses all creation.

Resurrection

Joy is overtaking me,
Every crevice of my Soul;
"Why not!" my limitless recipe
Fills what was once a beggar's bowl.

B. Elizabeth Atkinson

I began to ponder what I'd written about bliss, I thought about how often bliss and awakening seemed to be about some "perfected" state. I couldn't see that, even as I read it in some spiritual literature. I had the idea of perfection deep within me. I didn't fully embrace accepting my imperfect self until I wrote the "Enough" poem. Even then, it was only the beginning. I often found that I learned the same lesson several times, only each time it went deeper, like the preverbal peeling the layers of an onion.

Months later, out of that questioning, came this paper. As you'll notice, these Bliss Paper writings often came in the form of "teachings" that employ the pronouns we and our. Maybe they were always meant to be shared. This paper is a prime example of that teaching style.

Bliss is Not Perfection

Birth and death are opposites, *not* life and death. *Life* is infinite Being.

Many of us in the West are living our lives with an underlying desire for perfection—the perfect body, perfect job, perfect look, perfect spouse, perfect kids, perfect house and so on. Even when we outwardly protest this idea, it is often just below the surface and feeds the insecurity that what we are and what we have is "less than" whatever our idea of perfection is.

Intellectually we grasp that no one is perfect, yet everything in our consumer driven world and its daily advertising bombards us with the idea that perfection is attainable if we'd only do more or buy more. Many of us live as consumers who accumulate things to feel better about our lives. We don't realize that what we really need to consume and acknowledge is our divinity within.

Psychology supports the idea that no one is perfect and seeks to assist us in building a sense of self that is able to hold its own in the face of this ever-present bombardment of perfection. This can be a helpful step, but still we may be left struggling - spirit held at bay in a world of duality - since spirituality and leading a symbolic life can go unaddressed in many therapies.

And so, when we read about states of Bliss in spiritual literature, the idea of perfection might come to mind, especially if it was used by the author, as in "reaching a *perfected* state," liking it to an ending. This is because Bliss sounds like what we associate with perfection. We may think perfection comes from chasing after good and running away from bad. That's because perfection is part of the duality we assume is *Life*: perfect/imperfect; good/bad; male/female; right/wrong; heaven/earth, and so on.

It is also subjective. Just as with good and bad, what you describe as perfect may be different from what I describe and certainly different cultures would describe it differently. The truth is, there is no such thing as perfect; it is just a subjective judgment. Duality and the limitations of vocabulary force us into subjective judgment and a lack of compassion, thereby keeping us separate from the other.

It's not perfection we are seeking, but wholeness and it comes only by embracing our imperfections as a part of the whole, not running from, hiding or banishing them. Embracing imperfection leads us to embrace it in all people and things and to find true compassion. Rather than the dualities of life, which include perfection, Bliss is about being in present moment harmony with the fullness of *Life*—all that exists.

What do I mean by *Life*? *Life* is wholeness, the totality of being present to each moment. The two opposite poles of the psyche are transformed by integration and open to an infinite, vibrant, steady stream of learning and growth—not just the growth of our physical body and intellect, but the *expanding of our consciousness*. (This is what we call *evolution* and applies to everything on and in the earth. When bacteria, for instance, become resistant to antibiotics, they have expanded their "consciousness" and made physical changes to correspond with that expansion.)

We see our bodies and minds grow from childhood to old age and all the stages in between, yet we do not fully realize the degree to which our consciousness can grow, and that *this growth needs the same level of care and attention as our physical body*; we need to awaken to this awareness. It is this process of awakening to Bliss, that does have an end—an end to the *process* of integration, not to the steady stream of learning.

When we come into harmony with *All That Is*, you experience a continuous reverence for *Life*. Through compassionate love, gratitude and acceptance of what is, you no longer resist. A tipping point is reached where we live in the moment, flow with *Life*, and trust Wisdom. This is grounded Bliss. Consciousness continues to expand and learn which brings new information. There is *no struggle*: when we no longer experience our self as separate or identify with duality, there is no resistance, nothing to bump up against—like good struggling as it bumps up against bad.

It's not that we are immune from experiencing difficulties; it's that we accept them and *respond* rather than *react*. We are not only evolving our consciousness, but the collective consciousness as well. Our life looks ordinary from the outside, but we are living the life we are given in each moment.

Doubting ourselves, the Higher Self within, is at the root of all resistance. And there is a significant period of time during this process where much clearing of the psyche and its projections must be done in order for us to *discern and know* clearly and to *trust* what we know. For most of us, it is shrouded in debris, which hampers discernment, and we become frustrated by pundits saying "the answers are within."

We think, "Then why am I in this predicament?" We are "in this predicament" because our ability to see the answers clearly can be clouded and distorted by our misperceptions. That's why it's said, "be careful what you ask for" because we often get what we want, yet may find it's not so great after all, those unconscious distortions effecting our desire.

Even so, these misperceptions always place us in situations where we have an opportunity to learn where we are blocked, conflicted and not meeting our needs. We can choose to see this as information to elicit change and move on or pummel ourselves for our mistakes, labeling ourselves victims. Most of us have experienced moments of clarity that we acted on and they remind us that such clarity does indeed exist.

When we consciously make an agreement with ourselves to awaken and say "Yes!" to *Life*, grace comes to meet us. We embark on a process of self-discovery, self-acceptance and loving kindness which culminates in an end to our identity with duality and the struggle between those two poles. We now learn with ease and in peace. The ultimate choice of free will is whether to grow in duality trying to find perfection or whether to stop resisting and grow into the fullness of *Life* which is Bliss.

Skinny Girl

When I was a skinny little girl dressed in a skirt and blouse from the "Bargain City" store, I would cinch my belt as tight as I could stand it, the extra leather dangling down my skirt. I thought I wasn't OK. I thought I was fat.

When I took a second helping, a chorus of voices and chortles would rise from the dinner table, "You're going to be just like Aunt Margarite," my obese aunt who had come to visit once. My siblings teasing voices continued, my parents affirming them.

No one person was to blame; kindness wasn't a prevailing theme at dinnertime in our home. It just happened. What did we know; we were just kids. I had a normal body. I was OK. What did I know; I was just a kid.

So, every day I woke up and cinched my belt.

My friends tried to stop me - it bunched my blouse; it looked very uncomfortable. I didn't listen. The voices of doom had spoken.

My relationship to food and the dinner
table has never been the same.

I'd cinch my belt if I thought it would help.

B. Elizabeth Atkinson

I started to notice around this time that I was still having trouble with my new lifestyle. In the late 90's, I had moved away from San Francisco and into my parent's home. I can't recall what I said to them that would make this OK. It wasn't the truth. The truth was I'd been waking up for several months with words telling me I needed to move to my parent's home. I didn't want to do that. No way. I'd been on my own for many years, so I ignored the message.

Then after 3-4 months of this, I had a premonition that my dad would die - found myself spontaneously writing his obituary one morning even though he wasn't ill - and it pushed me to stop resisting this message about moving. I was flying a bit blind. I stored my furniture and moved to their home, which was in another city. I felt a bit lost without my work and income. I had enough money for a while, but what was I going to do? Who was I without my profession? What would people think of me, living with my parents? I had a long period of adjustment with the SAL experience and its impact on my life. (When I eventually read that Gopi Krishna couldn't continue his work for a long time after his awakening, that was helpful for me to know.)

I thought my dad would pass in about six months; it was nine months. I wondered if my premonition was accurate during those first months. Although there was no prolonged illness, I started noticing certain "closure" behavior from my dad around six months after arriving. I figured it wouldn't be much longer, and it wasn't. Although always accurate, intuitive thoughts and premonitions don't come with much detail - we may find ourselves filling in that detail with guesswork and timing that is often incorrect. Dad became ill and died in less than 24 hours.

So now what? All I had was "move to your parent's." A few weeks after the funeral, I told my mother I would need to go back to SF, that my money was running out; I had been paying rent and my own food, etc. She asked me to stay. She said she'd give me a "stipend." I knew this would make me vulnerable, but also saw that it would ease her mind. I told her I wanted to go away for a few days to a little town not too far to think about her offer.

As I pondered the offer, I realized that staying would also help me since I still didn't know what was happening with me, still hadn't heard of the Indian term, kundalini. Also, it was a very active time for the SAL -- energy buzzing all over, other people feeling it from me without any conscious intention on my part and a lot of emotion. Even in that honeymoon year in San Francisco, my ability to work in my profession was proving a challenge. Helping my mother benefitted me, too.

I struggled those three days knowing how very vulnerable I'd be depending on this "work-stipend," but I finally decided to stay. It was not an easy decision in its execution. I was judged by my siblings. I could understand their dismay; I felt it. I also judged myself. Even for my mother, who wanted me there, I was not a favorite. It took a while for her to accept me. Due to all of this, it was not a supportive atmosphere.

I learned a lot from these years of struggle in my new surroundings. I'd say it was 50% wonder and awe about what I was experiencing and 50% emotional struggle and deep, insightful learning. Being harshly judged by my siblings, especially one nearby, and negatively judging myself took a heavy toll. I was dealing with what Eckert Tolle calls the pain body.

I haven't encountered struggle, resistance, for a number of years now, but I continue to learn. It was during those long years of varying degrees of resistance that I wrote the poem you'll read soon, "Enough," and the following essay.

Accepting Ourselves

"This above all, to thine own self be true." Shakespeare

"To know what you prefer instead of humbly saying amen to what the world tells you, you ought to prefer is to have kept your soul alive." Robert Louis Stevenson

"The hope of a secure and livable world lies with disciplined nonconformists who are dedicated to justice, peace, and brotherhood." Martin Luther King, Jr.

There are those of us who feel a bit different and outside the mainstream of thought during this process of awakening and perhaps there is little understanding from some of our family or friends. A spiritual experience and its inquiry can thrust us into lifestyle changes with perceptions that are not yet universally acknowledged or accepted. As we adjust and come to terms with what is happening to us, we must recognize that just as important as finding a community of tolerant and like-minded folk, it is important to know this: *there is value in being on the periphery, just as there is value in the mainstream. It is the periphery that shapes and influences the direction of the mainstream, just as a flowing river is shaped by its borders, the riverbanks.*

There is a tremendous force to the rushing river of mainstream: the pull to think like, act like, be like and conform to its mind-set and values in order to be accepted. We recognize that there is great value to this rushing flow of mainstream: it carries life, our heritage and provides practicality and sustenance.

It is enriched by what has been, is and will be as the water moves onward — stretching, changing and moving to the nuances of its environment. And what shapes that environment? The periphery does. What would happen if the banks of the river did not "stand its ground," if it succumbed to the rushing force and tumbled into the river? Soon that swift current of water would be going nowhere — one, big, stagnant pool of swirling debris.

The periphery feeds the river with its varied self: like the riverbank full of sticks, leaves, rocks, fungus, insects and a multitude of plants and organisms in various stages of life and decay. On occasion, the influence of the periphery is so strong, a particular area finds itself overtaken, no longer part of the border; the great river reached out, overtook, and fully incorporated it into itself as it rushed along.

In all its variations, whether large or small, the periphery shapes, directs, nurtures and influences the mainstream so it is ever changing, ever renewed, ever provided with opportunities to move this way or that, pool or bubble, cleanse or create on its way to integration with the Sea. When we look at the river, we automatically take in its borders; there is not one without the other. They are a whole and so it is with us.

It is an apt analogy, reminding us that whether we find ourselves in the mainstream or on the periphery, our role is valued—an important part of the whole, a needed and purposeful participation that adds to creation. Many great artists, writers, scientists, musicians, ordinary individuals and groups who challenged the status quo were non-conforming in their contribution, mavericks and on the periphery. We would be lost without them. They shaped and influenced the river of life profoundly and continue to do so.

Never underestimate your value in the world. The web of life would suffer from your absence.

Maybe you directly touch thousands or, more likely, just a few. If you could see the big picture, you would know that those few you touch may go on to touch others who influence others, and so on — all intricately linked. On the road to integration, we must let go of the fear of not belonging, forgive ourselves and others (accepting what is) and be sincere to who we are and the role we play in this great opera of life. As author Joan Chittister so eloquently states in her book, <u>There is a Season</u>:

> *"Without the inner freedom it takes to defy the chains of convention, without the self-esteem it takes to trust our own truth, we face our worlds unprepared and unaware. Freedom is the capstone of truth. Our time is short here and there is much to do. Therefore, we must cultivate a passion for the truth. We must seek it, demand it and tell it. And once we have broken through the levels of propriety and protocol that collude to pretend that what isn't true is necessary, we are forever free. No one can enslave us again.*

> *"Self-esteem is the blessing that comes with honesty. With self-esteem we cannot lose, no matter what we lose. Longfellow's lines hold immortal value: 'Those that respect themselves are safe from others; they wear a coat of mail that none can pierce.' When we have done what must be done, what we were put here to do at this time, in this age, at this place, then we can live with heads up and hearts unbroken, whatever our losses. Then no one can best us, even when we fail the fray. Then we will never die before we have lived."*

What Do You Say?

And what do you say about victimhood, about feeling "put upon" when it's clear everyone was just vying for love – vying for love like there was only so much to go around, like if you didn't get yours, it would be as empty as that ice cream container left in the fridge, as though life was limited in its abundance, as though you must guard yourself against those who would take your portion, or run away with it and leave you with the pain of emptiness so you don't want to love anymore. What do you say when no one wants to look in, so they project out?

You remember your own imperfections and say, I forgive you and I forgive myself.

B. Elizabeth Atkinson

Enough

Today I decided I am enough.
For a long time, I spoke about
healing--that I needed to heal
or others needed to heal.
I read about healing, went to bookstores
filled with spiritual
treatises by able teachers:
"Heal," they said.

Teachers and authors abound and
call us to heal our body, mind and spirit.
So much to do; there was no end
to the imperfections I could find.
Just when I thought I might
be saint-like at last,
another reminder would come that
showed me my foibles and
there I'd be, another imperfection to heal.

So one day I woke up and thought: I've had enough.
I have had enough!
Regardless of any imperfections,
I am full of love, full of desire
to "do the right thing,"
wish no person ill, and do not want

to be the source of anyone
thinking badly about themselves.
Perhaps I do not fully succeed in this,
and my imperfections impede my desires.
Even so, I a m e n o u g h.

Thy mystery is in the paradoxes of *Life*,
and the mystery that is me,
embodies the paradox of Thee.
So today, I have decided: I a m e n o u g h.
I stand before my Self – a bouquet of flowers in hand,
love emblazoned in every cell – and
I embrace All That I Am.
Arms entwined, I s h a l l n e v e r l e t y o u g o.

I sit resplendent in nature
Not knowing where I begin and *it*
leaves off nor where *it*
begins and I end.
I am the grass the trees and the land.
I am the pond and the ocean.
I look up and see that I am that hill
and those mountains, and
just like you.
I am the softness of the breeze, the deep
sky and the meandering clouds.
I shine with the stars and warmly
nurture this earth with the
glistening sun.
I even wax and wane with the moon,
and, like her, am ever constant.

I come to fullness, then wait to be reborn.
I am enough.

B. Elizabeth Atkinson, 2005

I spent the first few years with my mother being somewhat reclusive; I felt like a cloistered nun. Since she smoked for most years I lived there, and could become unpleasant during her cocktail hour, my domain became my upstairs rooms. There was little plant growth around. All I could see from the one window in my bedroom was the side of a building, the tops of roofs and some sky.

In that small room, I positioned a mirror across from my bed, so I could see a lovely olive tree that shouldered the street. It was small at the time, but grew with me. I could see when its leaves sashayed in the light. I loved that tree. It was my touchstone for years.

When I wrote, pondered or contemplated life, or when I just gazed, that tree held my eyes. Her swaying branches and leaves let me know the strength of the wind that day and reflected her rootedness and the peace of nature. She signified life and aliveness for me. We were in relationship. Trees, and nature in general, still provide that love and focus for me.

I read and wrote madly in that bedroom and contemplated all that I was experiencing and everything around me. I was continuously curious and driven by this desire to know. I thought about how I was thinking of my spiritual path as something separate, how I heard others use language that verbally demonstrated this disconnect.

When I was questioning anything like this in my thoughts or simply wondering about it, another spontaneous, intuitive paper might come like this one. The writing was continuing to come through me and teach me.

Life is The Spiritual Journey

"Bidden or unbidden, God is present."
A plaque over Jung's doorway

Life *and* the spiritual journey, that's how we usually express it. We often talk about our spiritual journey as something different or separate from our everyday life. We separate soul and science, and regularly use words of duality and separateness: good/bad; right/wrong; perfect/imperfect; heaven/earth and now, <u>spiritual life versus everyday life.</u> Countless spiritual authors write about the necessity of reconnecting science and spirit; you've no doubt read about this over the years and it's become familiar. *What hasn't become familiar, and what we don't realize, is that we are still echoing the concept of separation with our very words and statements.*

LIFE *IS* THE SPIRITUAL JOURNEY! Learning through relationships (family, friends, coworkers) that what we judge in others, we harbor within ourselves, and learning what truly gives us joy *is* the spiritual journey. Learning to forgive and to love and accept ourselves by releasing resistance—this *is* spiritual. Allowing time for contemplation, learning to give and receive love, and to balance the seemingly disparate aspects of our lives, this *is* a holy life. It is fraught with meaning! We don't *try* to be spiritual; we *are* spiritual. The journey is simply becoming conscious of this fact and saying "Yes!" to *Life,* which changes our perceptions.

Think about the depth of this sentence: *We give time to that which we value.* So, when we speak words of separation by lamenting that we don't have enough time for our "spiritual" life, what we are really saying is: *I fear* taking time for my Self, honoring my Self, reflecting, meditating and becoming conscious (and so we devalue it). We abdicate our responsibility: it's the fault of too little time and those who demand our time. *We deny our power of choice.*

Life is one, infinite, vibrant, steady stream of learning, and *we* are responsible for our thoughts, words and actions. This is scary for many of us to contemplate. Yet abdication of this responsibility to the Self *always* creates struggle. We come into harmony with *Self*, with *Life*, when we release our resistance and embrace ourselves in love, thereby finding compassion and experiencing the joy of living in the present moment.

After I experienced a SAL, I read hundreds of books. I learned something from them all. Yet each time, especially in the early years, I was looking for *my* story. Although I never consciously said this, I think I was hoping that if I found *my* story, I could just follow it and everything would be easy, a snap – no thinking for myself, no errors of judgment, pain or whatever I feared. The way would be shown and that would be that.

Instead what I found were signposts, guiding words, but never *my* story. Each one of us is learning similar lessons; *we simply have our individual way of learning them.* We are given opportunities in our everyday lives and relationships to learn about ourselves and our projections over and over again.

We *choose to become conscious, to notice and welcome these lessons as a step closer to clarity*, not as an excuse to berate ourselves, which will bind us to our misguided thinking.

Nuns, monks, priests, rabbis, holy-men and women, gurus—in our respect for this way of life, we make the mistake of holding it up as a more spiritual life than our own. This is not so. Fortunately, the gifted of these people provide us with information, guide us and teach us, based on their extensive study of spiritual literature.

Only a small percentage of these people may be able to provide us a glimpse into evolved consciousness *based on their experience.* Which is to say, a life of celibacy, regimented ritual or being set apart is *one* way to learn about the spiritual, but is not *the* way and does not ensure an evolved consciousness that bespeaks the fullness of *Life.*

My dear friends, our own life is a meaningful, purposeful spiritual journey (and so is our neighbor's). Our life is the Way.

Mother Theresa won the Nobel Peace Prize because she established help for the poor, sick and dying, letting them know they were loved and embraced by God. She bespoke compassion and lived her life as a prayer challenging us with reminders of simplicity and purposefulness; we applaud this. It's also true that every day in the world, unsung people of passion, dedication and love are doing works of equal importance.

Perhaps we singled out Mother Theresa as a role model for her selfless work partly because she belonged to a celibate spiritual order, renounced material possessions and had no psychic associations. If so, it is important to note that these are not prerequisites to knowing All There Is/God or having compassion. What *is* necessary is to recognize that *the pursuit* of material possessions, sex, psychic phenomena and the like *as an end in themselves* can lead us astray, but they pose no harm in and of themselves.

What we are called to is *balance,* an integration of the dual poles of our psyche and simplifying the clutter in our lives; doing this through austerity is a choice, not a requirement. Our life is meaningful, infused with mystery and wonder, waiting to be acknowledged. As we grow into the knowledge and experience that we are all connected and, within our individuality, we interact with that *whole.* We no longer identify with dualism or feeling separate. This helps us move out of resistance and into the fullness of Life.

Because we have long-separated biological life and life of the spirit, we may seek out workshops, literature, religion and teachers to assist us in bridging the gap. I'm not suggesting otherwise. What I am suggesting is that we not make the mistake of seeing these endeavors as apart from what we learn in the vibrancy of our everyday lives. And further, that we realize that "bridging the gap" is all teaching does because ultimately the worth of any spiritual path or teacher is in their ability to lead us to our Self (inner Christ, Buddha, Goddess, Shakti, Light, etc.), our true teacher and guide.

Our creative insights and information that we discover must be woven into the fabric of our everyday life, felt in every cell of our body and grounded in the mundane. In this way our path is personalized, honoring our individual psyche and its heritage. The foundation is laid to awaken to the fullness of Life.

56

Reflection

Go on, go ahead.
Look into the mirror of your face.
There is not a spot nor a wrinkle
That is not imbued with My grace.

B. Elizabeth Atkinson

I had so many misconceptions early on. I began to realize as I dealt with my struggles over the years that there was more to all this than I'd thought. I might think one thing and counter it in my mind with another. I would feel confused and frustrated. It was all a conundrum. As always, when I was wondering about these misperceptions and difficulties, my pen met paper. Right off the bat this title told it all.

The Battle Within

> **"Our deepest fear is not that we are inadequate. Our deepest fear is that we are powerful beyond measure. It is our light, not our darkness that frightens us. We ask ourselves, who am I to be brilliant, gorgeous, talented and fabulous? Actually, who are you not to be? You are a child of God. Your playing small doesn't serve the world. There's nothing enlightened about shrinking so that other people won't feel insecure around you. We were born to manifest the glory of God within us. It's not just in some of us; it's in everyone. And as we let our own light shine, we unconsciously give other people the permission to do the same. As we are liberated from our own fear, our presence automatically liberates others."**

> **Marianne Williamson**
> **(quoted by Nelson Mandela at his inauguration)**

With women in particular, though not exclusively, an epidemic of low self-esteem and lack of worthiness festers within. I'm not talking about success and strength. We may be both successful and strong, a mainstream conformist or non-conformist, perceived with a solid, if vulnerable, strength.

Nevertheless, lurking beneath this "together" exterior is often the open wound of insecurity: *I am not enough - too this and too that.* This unhealed wound, out of fear of not being accepted and loved, too often tries to keep others happy by conforming and responding to what *they* want - an aberration of the "good mother" ideal of femininity. It remains unhealed by the inwardly turned anger of a child whose needs were not met, causing permeable or non-existent boundaries that extend into adulthood.

Unaware of how to express this seemingly inappropriate anger, it is contained within and festers as a deep, inner sadness of which we may or may not be aware. This sadness is also archetypal because victimization is based on the historical fear that we will be burned, staked, stoned or otherwise retaliated against (still occurring in some places) and because the feminine principle in our world cultures has been repressed for centuries. It's been projected onto females as being "less than," with a distorted and heightened responsibility for the feelings and actions of others and what they want, and feeling victimized because we're told it's "our fault."

We have taken in this distortion of the feminine and made it our own generation after generation. As a result, *we have learned not to trust ourselves.* (The same can be said for boys and men with an active feminine who, if they express it, can be considered soft or weak; often this weakness must be beaten down and drummed or bullied out for cultural and family acceptance.)

This sad anger often projects itself in outbursts of inner or outer blame, judgment, and victim-hood, never owning its source within. We may do various things to keep this knowledge hidden, strengthening our unawareness with excessive behavior of all kinds - be it binge eating, alcohol, drugs, minding other's business or being "terribly busy" (which allows one to bask in self-important image or outward success and negate any notion of sad anger within: "That's not me!"). Yet sad anger hungers to be acknowledged and embraced.

Ego (personality and who you *think* you are) resides in time and has a vested interest in keeping this the status quo. Its incessant thinking of past and future claim tyranny over the soul, utilizing a variety of tools to keep us in the dark: guilt, fear, inadequacy, imperfection, judgment, false pride and niceties, and a god of retribution to name a few. It fuels the thoughts that give voice to the inner "demons of negativity," nagging at us to give in to powerlessness (the mainstay of sad anger).

So, when you are committed to awakening Spirit within, *a battle may ensue.* Afraid it will lose out if it lets go, ego struggles to hold onto its supremacy; its old habits and fears may intensify now.

Fearful ego, as the inner saboteur, is trying to keep us unaware of the creative power within: our true, Divine Self and its unlimited potential. Power, ego is happy to remind us, is often associated with its misuse, hierarchy, retaliation, lack of femininity and being clothed in the anger of Machiavellian-like manipulation.

But rather than a negative force projected outward, sad anger can be transmuted to the authentic power of Love and used inwardly to fuel and strengthen our acceptance of self. This happens as we redirect our energy to challenge ego by refusing to sacrifice ourselves to its nagging voices *(talk back to them)*, recriminating judgment *(talk back to it)* victimhood *(talk back to it)*, and failure to meet our needs *(refuse to accept this)*.

By continually identifying with the love and forgiveness of the compassionate, divine feminine rather than ego, this nurturing mother within helps us learn to accept ourselves, to trust our inner voice and honor our needs, thereby ending ego's tyranny and the *reflexive* emotional reactions that served us in the past.

The paradox is that to access authentic power we must surrender *seeming* power – the power of ego's will (control); this is the sacrifice we are asked to make. It is rarely easy and always an act of humility. With the help of grace, we *allow* our true Self (inner Goddess, Christ, Buddha, etc.) which resides in the present moment to emerge and become one with the Divine. We identify with it rather than with ego. As Professor Michael Washburn states in <u>The Ego and the Dynamic Ground</u>, "*...ego as an instrument of spirit rather than spirit as a tool of ego.*"

This struggle can go on for a number of years, coming closer and closer to the surface of our consciousness. Our job is to trust *Life* and ourselves, and stay on the path of awareness, noticing the signs and signals that alert us when we stray off course.

We are guided again and again to the situations we need to resurrect the authentic power and love of the repressed feminine. As we give voice to her nurturing love, support and trust, she subdues and balances our overabundant masculine and we are held in a cocoon of light.

These two poles of the psyche, masculine and feminine, now integrated as one, reside in present moment awareness and, with the Power of Love, awaken the full potential of our Divine Self: our individual, creative expression of *All There Is*.

~ Quiet Mind ~

Here is one of the ways harmony shows itself. It has to do with non-identification with your thoughts and emotions. Some of my thoughts quieted over time after the SAL, which means a lot of my emotion, too, because most emotion comes from thoughts. However, I didn't notice it until a few years ago when I was listening to Eckert Tolle. He said something about listening to someone speak about the quiet mind and he realized about 80% of his thoughts were gone.

As I listened to him, I had the same experience he had. I tuned in and realized the same was true for me, about 80% less chatter than before. When the other 20%

showed themselves, it was up to me not to attach to those thoughts. I'm not always successful, but enough that my mind is fairly quiet.

This doesn't mean we never think. Obviously, we plan things and so forth. It just means all that judgmental, comparing, criticizing monkey mind chatter is nothing we need and dissipates over time. It doesn't mean we'll never feel grief or righteous anger or find ourselves in unpleasant, even unhappy situations. It means that somehow there is wisdom in a still mind: the answers or way is shown.

Responses come to us in this stillness and we learn to trust them. We get out of the driver's seat and trust that the Universe, in its own time, will bring us what we need (though perhaps not always what we think we want).

~ Trust and Hope ~

Hope can move us forward and provide solace in difficult times, yet embedded in hope is the fear that, really, we may not be able to manifest what we want. It is a *wish* for benevolence, not a *trust* that it exists. Trust comes from *knowing* the Universe is friendly and being receptive to it. We might hope for this or that, but hope does not supersede trust. We must trust *Life* even if some of our hopes don't transpire. Trust is knowing the power of not-knowing, the certainty of uncertainty and the miracle of the present moment: Now. With trust we embrace the unknown, the mystery of All There Is. It is our only certainty.

I was beginning to read about the two poles of the psyche in Michael Washburn's Transpersonal Theory book, <u>The Ego and The Dynamic Ground</u>, and hearing non-duality terms and Buddhist teachings about the middle way, etc. I wondered what this meant in my everyday life, this middle way or still point? And what was non-duality? I was still understanding things more intellectually than experientially. For me, emotional struggle lingered.

Standing in the Still Point
of the Opposites

"When you make the two one, and when you make the inner as the outer and the outer as the inner, and the above as the below, and when you make the male and female into a single one — then shall you enter the Kingdom." Jesus in the Gospel of St. Thomas

"The human mind rarely sees beyond these opposites to the Greater Unity that necessitates them. But the mind can awaken to Greater Unity, and in this lies the purpose of Creation and of humankind." Reb Yerachmiel ben Yisrael

Over and over again we hear or read about the term duality in certain spiritual literature. Intellectually, we understand what the word means, but we may not fully internalize its meaning.

The unabridged edition of the *Random House Dictionary of the English Language* states that duality (as a state of being dual) means having a two-fold, or double, character or nature. Note that in this definition, the "character or nature" of something is single, one thing, while dual describes this oneness as being two-fold. In other words, two sides of the same coin. Using this metaphor, *Life*, wholeness, is the coin, while all the aspects of duality that we associate with mundane life — right/wrong; heaven/earth; perfect/imperfect; good/ bad; question/answer, me/you; birth/death are the two sides.

Neither side of the coin of *Life* makes up the whole coin. Yet what do you get when you acknowledge and combine the two sides? You get Divine paradox because the sum (the *still point*) is greater than its parts.

> Combine right and wrong and you find **Compassion**.
> Add love and hate and you come to **Forgiveness**.
> Combine good and bad and you have **Non-judgment**.
> Combine male and female and you achieve **Balance**.
> Surrender control and you birth **Creative Expression**.
> Combine hope and despair and you discover **Trust**.
> Bring Heaven to Earth and you find **Peace**.

The nature of the Divine, The Unknown, is couched in this paradox and told in the language of metaphor and myth. This is why we can become befuddled in our attempt to understand everything with the intellect. But with this nature, Divine Mystery is not captured within one definitive belief system; it provides for many paths.

Regardless of our path, we honor Spirit by "showing up for Life," i.e., being present as we accept what is, including all parts of ourselves. We can choose to see only one side of the coin at any given moment or we can begin to see the coin as a whole and reap the benefits of Divine paradox. The choice is ours and ours alone.

To see *Life* as a whole changes our perception. It doesn't mean we are blind to the perception of duality around us. We *acknowledge the emotions of* happy and sad, the judgments of good and bad, *but we no longer identify ourselves with either.* We align and identify ourselves with the center *still point* which encompasses all the opposites, is divinely inspired and full of paradox. In this *still point*, which accepts each moment as it is, we *participate* with Life because everything is a part *of* God, *in* God and participates *as* God, i.e., All There Is.

Even so, God is more than the sum of Its parts—Divine paradox again. The ultimate duality is God/Self; transform consciousness and this duality becomes a unified whole—you are not separate from All That Is. When we pray *to* something, *we pray to that part of ourselves of which we are not yet conscious.* Standing in the *still point*, your life can *be* the prayer.

Our usual concept of who we are includes duality; this causes struggle as we identify with one side of the coin or another - we are in resistance. Yet, we can make the choice to allow what is and acknowledge Love, the Divine, in each moment. (This isn't about passivity-- clearly you vote for one or another candidate, may work to make the world a more equitable place and may desire change in your life. This is about accepting what is in any given moment *even as you work for desired change.*)

In that *still point* we awaken to the fullness and joy of Life. We continue learning as consciousness continues to expand, but we *no longer learn through struggle.* Our purpose is to recognize and accept the wholeness of each moment, to *re-member* Spirit in this, our sacred and symbolic life. Odd as it sounds, there is nothing you need to "do" really, no practice, because you are whole *now;* you are okay right *now.* Of course, most of us don't recognize this, therefore we embark on a spiritual journey or process to realize these truths.

I'm not suggesting this recognition happens with speed and ease, although it can. To look within and accept our own foibles and pitfalls, to see our wholeness and move out of the mainstream of thought is an act of courage. It's one thing to intellectually get the concept of non-duality--that you are whole *now*, just as you are. It's usually quite another to truly embody that concept by experiencing and living it. It's not an end you can make happen; there is grace involved.

Yet this evolution of consciousness is our heritage. It is a process as real as the physical evolution of our bodies and brains. Side by side, the physical and unseen have shared a process of evolutionary learning—expanding in conscious wisdom and expanding in physical adaptation based on that consciousness. There is a genetics of consciousness just as real as our physical genetics, and this radically effects our awakening process - *how we experience Spirit is within the context of our individuality.* Nevertheless, the goal is the same—to stand in the *Still point* of the opposites, fully accepting ourselves and Life as it is in each moment. This surrender opens the door for you to experience a *state* of love.

~ The State of Love ~

There is a state of love, just as there exists emotional love. The state of love is our default state; when we opt to identify with our thoughts and emotions, we override this default using will/ego. The State of Love is God, Being, All There Is, etc., and resides in the present moment. We touch it now and then and eventually sustain it for longer periods of time. It is this State of Love with which we are asked to identify, i.e., I *am* Love. Yes, I have a body, a highly sensitive, empathic nature, a personality, but none of these things *are* me: I *have* them.

As part of duality, emotional love has conditions: is it good or bad; do I like it or not; is it pleasing or not? Love/hate. Non-judgmental, compassionate love is a condition of the State of Love. (It is not the same as feeling sorry for someone or thing; again, it is not emotional love and does not feel the same.)

The State of Love exists within us, infused with gratefulness, and gracefully arises as we let go of resistance and live in the moment. It slowly overtakes our entire being. Even as it was always us, we feel like it *becomes us.* This State of Love exists outside of duality. It is; as such, it is ever-present and eternal outside of any prerequisites, yet encompassing them all. This is who we really are--not our thoughts, not our emotions or judgments, but this calm, intelligent ever-present love.

This next paper came as I pondered the writings of Peace Pilgrim, a woman who didn't use the word enlightened about herself, but defined her state as "an end to struggle." She wrote how she never stopped learning - just that she didn't have to do it through struggle [resistance] anymore. I use that terminology all the time; it's simple and easy to understand. She also talked about being unshakeable and I wondered what that meant. I began to write.

What I Mean by Doubt and Being Unshakable

"What lies behind us and what lies before us are small matters compared to what lies within us." Emerson

Being "unshakeable in all things" means an end to all doubt. Now you may protest at first that this sounds like self-righteousness, someone who always thinks they are right about everything. This is because our mind jumps back to duality — right/wrong — and associates the idea of doubt with this duality. "There's no doubt about it!" we say when we're sure we're right.

I'm talking about doubt on a larger scale where *in a consistently expanded state* we no longer question the moment. We are in such harmony with the flow of *Life*, with being, that we allow each moment to be as it is, not as we think it should be, and we meet it with grace. Every aspect of our lives has come into this harmony — our thoughts, words and actions, even our jobs and relationships.

This doesn't mean things are perfect; it means we are in harmony with what is. With integration, we see that all is well and there is no need to be reactive, i.e., defensive, which is fear-based resistance and includes fearing death.

Undifferentiated from All There Is, we know in the marrow of our bones that our individual life is meaningful and purposeful, even when we don't see the immediate results of our actions. This experiential knowing makes us unshakeable in all things. Even as we have an intention for how our life will be and move in that direction, we realize nothing needs to be forced and changes are inevitable. We come to this understanding:

> I don't need to try to
> make something happen.
> It happens spontaneously.
> It rises out of its own accord,
> Its own need to be created;
> And it happens in the moment,
> As *Life* presents its possibilities —
> As what is created presents itself.
> This is the essence of nature.

This doesn't mean we never encounter difficult situations or people. It means when we are presented with a difficult situation, we are also presented with everything we need—the complete wherewithal—to handle it in the very moment it appears - the clarity of integration. As an innate part of the ego, fear can block these abilities on the path to integration; ego thinks it is separate from All There Is and fears the loss of control. Development of the ego is an important stage in growth, yet if we continue to identify with it and its separateness; we experience doubt, the struggle of duality, and are afraid we may be overwhelmed by the perceived difficulties of becoming consciousness and knowing our Truth.

Yet, in a sustained, abiding state of awakening where we learn without struggle, we interact in harmony with the Universe, with All There Is, whatever the emotion and challenge. Ego gives way to Spirit as it realizes its participation and non-separation from all *Life*.

In the simple act of *allowing*, our resistance dissipates and *life becomes effortless* (ego in service to Spirit). It flows freely and the knowledge, wisdom and necessities for any given circumstance are met in that moment.

Experiencing this, we become unshakeable. There is no doubt. Our intentions flow from those of the Universe.

As Deepak Chopra notes, "Intent in nature orchestrates its own fulfillment...in actuality people who are connected with the conscious intelligence field adopt the intentions of the universe. Their intentions are being met...because the cosmic mind is using their intentions to fulfill its own desires."

One of my biggest struggles was trying to love everyone in the way I thought I was reading about or hearing in spiritual lectures. While I liked most everyone, and certainly didn't hate anyone, I thought I must be deficient or remiss because this emotional loving of everyone didn't always work for me. It became another reason to judge myself.

Loving everyone didn't work because my concept of love was wrong. I taught myself about loving others and myself as the following paper came through me. I never knew what the next sentence was going to be, but it made sense and helped me immensely.

Open Your Heart and I Am There

"The only internal relationship anyone ever has is with the higher Self... Self-love grows when you refuse to follow the impulses of anger and fear, trust that the universe is on your side, form your desires from the heart and watch the higher Self carry them out, believe that you are enough in and of yourself... put your attention on positive energies in every situation, honor your own needs without having to seek outside approval, and cultivate the peace of inner silence." Deepak Chopra

Most of us equate an open heart with love, unconditional love being its highest form. I suggest that an open heart is not an outpouring of emotion-filled sentimental love toward everyone (which can lend itself to condoning mistreatment of ourselves while excusing unacceptable behavior). Rather, an open heart is a grateful heart; it *receives* love by releasing resistance — the resistance we have to forgiving ourselves and others, thereby accepting *self*-love and gratitude for *All There Is.*

This sets the stage for unconditional love, a love not clearly understood. *Unconditional, compassionate love is without malice, accepting ourselves and others as they are. We desire only what's best for them.* It's a love that comes through the discerning solar plexus, and is then expressed through the heart; on its own, the heart can be *led* by emotion. Therein lies the confusion. A *pure* heart works in concert with the intuitive, discerning solar plexus. *

Emotions can help us form attractions and bonds to a partner, our children, our culture, and the beauty around us. Nevertheless, emotions can be picked up from others, be distorted by inner shadows and sidelined from conscious living via our emotionally repressive habits. These can *lead* love to express itself as zeal and projected angst allowing us to follow harsh dictators (both without and within), national and cultural aggression and misinterpreted religious beliefs that persecute others in the name of Love, God, Allah, or the like.

Even though we may deeply love our spouse, children, and friends, many of us have tossed judgments or verbal assaults their way at one time or another (or repressed them into self-loathing). In themselves, the universal language of emotions acts as inner messengers with information to be valued. Though we may have been taught not to identify with our thoughts; it's also true that we are not our emotions.

We *are called to identify with our Divine nature, our true Self, not our ego/personality.* We *have* a personality; it isn't who we are. By attaching to emotion — identifying with it — we look for a reason to explain why we're feeling it, sometimes projecting it onto others which gives form to shadow. This is *reacting* rather than *responding* to what these non-judgmental emotions are trying to tell us (empathic information): they're *emotions leading as opposed to emotions informing.*

How do we reconcile these disparities of love? By releasing resistance and recognizing that *compassionate love is a by-product of self-love, the doorway leading to it.* When we open our heart with gratefulness and give way to forgiving, accepting, and loving ourselves, we receive the power of grace that has been waiting for us: the blossoming of the higher Self (inner Christ, Buddha, Goddess, etc.). Then, and only then, are we capable of compassionate love. We express the divinity and harmony that lives in everyone and pervades all life. Ego no longer runs the show; it is now in service to Spirit.

This self-love necessitates an end to the inner struggle of ego-in-charge, the cause of distress in all of us (because ego is unable to detach from the outcome or wanting control). Whether our bodies are healthy, diseased or otherwise suffering, releasing resistance to this grateful love of forgiveness brings us peace. It is the whole point of the inner journey; all woes boil down to its suppression. It entails facing and embracing our fears, negative habit-thinking, regrets and denials, and taking full responsibility for ourselves: no victim thinking, martyr behavior, projected angst or ego inflation.

When we take responsibility for ourselves by opening our heart, we stop chasing imperfections, accept what is, are grateful for life and recognize we are enough. (This is not resignation; accepting what is brings about an opening for change, movement and transformation.) A kind of grace intervenes and we hold ourselves in the embrace of loving kindness.

This grace awakens the wisdom and creative power of the non-dual Self, a wonder to behold. Accepting what is (ourselves as we are; the situation as it stands) without judgment or attachment to the outcome, allows the Self to be liberated and take the lead; it is a recognition of *ego's powerlessness to end the inner struggle. This recognition is what is meant by humility.*

Until our own inner work is done, we often meet others at the level of our misperceptions and wounds, thereby having the opportunity to move ourselves into harmony. Then, as we become more aligned with Spirit, we begin to meet others with Divine clarity. We're no longer sidetracked by the distortions of the other; rather through compassion, we see the Divine Light in the other.

This is where we connect. This is where all harmonizing occurs. The grateful love that emanates from a resurrected Self can do no less than recognize its reflection in everything else. It is our innate nature: how we see and treat ourselves is reflected in how we see and treat others. We often give ourselves away by what we criticize, harshly judge and find fault with in others. If we hold other's feet to the fire, how our own feet must burn with self-judgment and recrimination, whether conscious or deeply buried.

At the same time, it is healthy and normal to discern with whom we feel comfortable and wish to spend time, and with whom we don't. Even in families, we may find we have an attachment of birth, but not an intimacy of loving kindness; we may even be called to walk away. *It is not that we have a "kinship of personality" with all whom we encounter. Rather, what we recognize and acknowledge is our "kinship of Spirit."*

As we release resistance to accepting and loving ourselves, our hearts are opened to receive the grace of compassion influenced by the discerning solar plexus. That compassion allows us to move out of reaction and realize, just as we did with ourselves, that the wrong turns, unkindness, even brutalities, put forward by others are based on their own self-judgments, distortions and suppressed hurts projected outward — we can forgive others even as we hold them accountable for their actions (*i.e., we may respect someone as a spiritual being, but not respect their actions as a human being*).

With a *pure* heart - gut and heart in concert - we cease to attract negativity, and with grace and luck open the door further to the peaceful embrace of the ever present, non-dual state of love.

* The solar plexus is both a spiritual energy center in many belief systems and scientifically has been found to house many nerve receptors. A network of nerves in your belly is in constant communication with your brain; it's often referred to as the brain in the gut. Professor Kevin Olden, MD, notes "Gut feelings are a very definite form of information...called the enteric system, it contains over 100 million neurons. That's more than the spinal cord." UCLA gastroenterologist, Emeran Mayer, theorizes that, "As much as 80% of our well-being might come from the complicated interplay between the brain in our head and the one in our gut." See the TED Fulbright YouTube video, "Food for Thought: How your belly controls your brain" by Ruari Robertson

It wasn't until this last paper that I began to see that all the essays I had written, taken together, were my own personalized, spiritual path. I can remember the exact moment I looked at this essay and had that insight. It's when I gave the papers the title, The Bliss Papers. It's interesting to note that many of these concepts I wrote about, especially in this essay, were long before I really embodied any of them. I don't know how I knew what I wrote about, although a few concepts I'd probably read about in some form or another. I taught myself through this writing, well before I understood it all.

My interest in the science of my experience is alluded to in this paper. Although I experienced much more phenomena than I've relayed in these papers, I want to tell you about another one I experienced. I was awakened in the middle of the night. It was dark and I was hearing what I thought was some kind of radio - except I realized there was no radio in my room nor in any of the rooms close to mine. Nothing was coming from the outdoors.

I soon realized I was hearing the "radio" voice inside my head. It was a male voice, unknown to me. He had been talking the whole time I was trying to determine what was going on. My thoughts being elsewhere, I didn't know what he was saying.

His last words were something like, "Ask your angels about King Mufuso." I'm not sure of the exact word he used (but I think it was Mufuso) because I was so focused on where this voice was coming from. This was the only time I actually heard a voice like that speak to me inside my head. Was this akin to the voices some mentally ill people hear? A spirit of sorts? I don't know.

Please ask yourself, as I have so often asked myself, how could these examples of phenomena I outline in these papers manifest in a person's body? What is going on biologically? There must be a science behind it; call it a "biology of spirit" for now. Though I may not be a scientist, I am a very curious observer.

When repeated phenomena are not part of a culture's accepted science, they become anecdotal and explained via spiritual or psychic belief systems; mainstream science doesn't take them seriously.

Yet, the light experience I'm calling a SAL happened. I didn't imagine it. A SAL has properties, side effects if you will, that open the door to biological phenomena and seeing the world less egotistically. It changed and expanded my biology in ways I may never know, and it's happened to many people over the millennium.

Experiences of light are absolutely real. Nevertheless, due to scientific skepticism, I and others experience these changes brought on by a SAL in a culture that pushes them to the sidelines, sometimes with a chuckle. Most of us who've had experiences of light and phenomena are ordinary and remain unknown.

In the separation of science and spirit, we've thrown out the baby with the bathwater. Not accepted as a legitimate field of study, mystical experience sits on the sidelines of mainstream science when it could be providing new tools and amazing insights into our evolutionary biology.

After all, science and spirit meet at the doorway to wonder - scientists try to explain it; mystics experience it. As Diane Ackerman poetically writes, "Wonder is the heaviest element on the periodic table. Even a tiny fleck of it stops time."

Mystery is like ever-expanding concentric circles waiting for new discoveries that cause us to break through to the next circle. There are a few brave scientists and researchers who may already have an idea about these things, but little is accepted by the scientific mainstream. How limiting!

One day that will change. Research will expand beyond double-blind studies and answers will be found, explanations will come. On that day, spirituality will embrace new mystery, and those answers will generate new questions, maybe even from someone as ordinary as me.

Emptying Ourselves Out

**You see things and say, "Why?" But I dream things that
never were and say, "Why not?"
George Bernard Shaw**

As humans we evoke ideas about how things work in our environment: take water for instance. We name it, then generate thoughts about its use and existence, and descriptions of its properties. Yet, to a fish, this is irrelevant. To her, water is experiential and a constant. There is not water as something apart from the fish; she breathes it. And such spirit asks of us.

The ultimate goal of any spiritual belief system is not the rote learning of its doctrine and following its rules; rather, it's experiential. We are called to evolve our consciousness to a point where grace intervenes and God (All There Is) is undifferentiated from ourselves and others. This state of love exists in the present moment.

Initially, I found that the left side of my brain was fully engaged in my quest to understand what was happening to me. This helped ground my experiences and keep them from overwhelming me. Yet, over time, I found it an obstacle: I was pressing to explain everything, including myself.

Again, and again, I discovered that in trying to dissect something, I limited it and hit a wall. Certain physiological things simply aren't known yet, and although I am a researcher of my own experience, I am not a scientist. With interest, curiosity and study, I can speculate and suggest, but a SAL or any awakening is by nature experiential and I sense I am here to express that experience. As Murray Bail writes:

> *"Once a given subject is broken down into parts, each one identified, named and placed into groups—the periodic table, strata of minerals, weight divisions of prizefighters—the whole is given limits and becomes acceptable, or digestible, almost. It may well be regarded as residual evidence of the oldest fear, the fear of the infinite. Anything to escape the darkness of the forest."*

Stripped of their dogma, bureaucracy, literalism and patriarchy all major religions are beautiful metaphors of the Infinite: stories and rituals that give form and meaning to the unexplainable, honor *Life* and allow our finite brain to wrap itself around purpose and mystery without limiting it.

I was inspired to reinterpret what I learned and compose a spiritual metaphor acceptable to my psyche, a bed on which the Infinite could rest. Because I was initially embarrassed by it all, didn't understand what the SAL was all about, I tried to *explain* the metaphor biologically and psychologically to find acceptance of my psychic experiences within our scientifically oriented society and, more importantly, within myself.

Although there are physical and psychological changes that come with an awakening, I also know it's only a hint at what lies in wait in our intent as we loosen our grip on the need to calm our fears by rehashing the past, worrying about the future or defending our experiences. Ego hides out in this incessant, time-oriented thinking hoping to continue its charade that it is our identity.

Yet, according to all the great mystical teachings, to live in the present moment is to find the Divine. Notes the 14th century Christian mystic Meister Eckhart, "Time is what keeps the light from reaching us. There is no greater obstacle to God than time." Rather than the ego-self, our identity resides in the non-dual Self of the present moment. That said, most of us find it a challenge.

For a while, towards the end of the SAL process (the end of resistance, but not of learning, wonder or even distress), it felt like I had one remaining hand grasped tightly around a fixed pole, ego (and its illusion of control) holding on for dear life, afraid of where it would be propelled if I lost my grip. I feared that to accept what is, and what I didn't want, would mean my desires would go by the wayside: seemingly emanating from ego, they would have to be sacrificed.

One by one my fingers were pried loose until finally my resistance slackened and a way for acceptance, surrender, and freedom was made; it took a long time for me. My fear was that by releasing my grasp on the reality I knew, I'd be thrown into a whirlwind—a hurricane or tornado—bandied about by overwhelming, perhaps violent, winds of change. I would lose myself and become desolate and isolated.

I found that as the winds of this battle within subside, the light of love overtakes this shadow of resistance at every level of our being. Just as a crying child surrenders to its hunger as its mother lifts it sweetly to her breast, so too, as we release our fears, the Divine *lifts* us with loving kindness into a nurturing state of pure calm, the *eye* of the storm. It is only then that we realize that we were holding onto the very "winds" we feared, and by letting go and allowing, we are carried to the place we always desired.

Even though we can set our *intention* and lay the groundwork, letting go is *not* an act of will—we can't *make* it happen; we *allow* it to happen when we can't bear the weight of resistance anymore (stage 4). It's then that a force of love *slowly* overtakes us. We come to reside in the peaceful eye of the storm, unshakeable, never again bandied about between the changing winds of duality. In this state of loving calm, we are in a perpetual dance with the fullness of *Life*. As Michael Washburn states in *The Ego and The Dynamic Ground*:

> *"Feelings, then, even very strong ones, do not ordinarily affect integrated people in a disruptive manner. Although easily touched, integrated people are rarely shaken, and although deeply moved, they are rarely swept away in emotional outpourings. To the untutored eye, it might even appear as though integrated people are unfeeling or uncaring.*
>
> *"Nothing could be further from the truth, however. For if the feelings of integrated people tend not to be loud, that is because they are so deep and true. Of course, in unhappy times integrated people are bound to experience the unhappiness of others. This sensitivity... gives rise to feelings of sadness and even mourning; it does not, however, make integrated people 'unhappy.'*

"Integrated people see, and therefore feel, both sides of life. Moreover, we should not forget that the feelings of blessedness and bliss are inherent to integrated existence. These feelings make up the affective ground of integrated existence, over which pass the pangs and pleasures, sufferings and joys of conscience. Although integrated people are keenly sensitive to the suffering of the world, they feel both an exquisite joy in being alive and an inexpressible gratitude for a world that, despite its serious flaws, is 'perfect.'"

I saw that in trying to scientifically explain my spiritual awakening by engaging my fearful ego, I hadn't fully surrendered to its mystery. In general, the more we know, the more there is to know; this is the infinite nature of the Cosmic Mind. Scientific discovery is a testament to creative expression and the evolution of consciousness and will be making great strides in the "biology of spirit." Yet mystery abides, and it is there so that we can let go and embrace reverence.

On the mystical path, I found I had to give up, give out, and give way—to pray the only prayer there is: "Yes!" Surrendering, even amidst fear and imperfection, releases Spirit to fully embrace me. I am free. I no longer dance *around* Life, but am joyfully and peacefully engaged *in* it. To live my life as a prayer is to *honor life with my total presence*, to be alive in each moment and let things happen effortlessly. As I live this life I am given, I become a mirror by which others can see themselves whole.

From <u>Searching for Stars on an Island in Maine</u> by theoretical physicist Alan Lightman

"I accept the idea that science and the scientific view of the world may not encompass all of existence. There could be realms of being outside the physical universe. We simple don't know what we don't know. And by definition, we would not be able to prove or disprove such nonphysical realms by methods or means within the physical universe.

"...they [qualities] will point back to a large family of noisy and feeling animals—the living, throbbing kingdom of life on our planet, of which we are a part. A kingdom that has never stood still but has changed and evolved and will always do so. A kingdom that consecrates life and its possibilities even as each of its individuals passes away. A kingdom that dreams of unity and permanence even as the world fractures and fades. A kingdom redesigning itself, as we humans now do. All is in flux and always has been. This is the thing I know, and perhaps the only thing that I know. Flux is beyond sadness and joy. Flux and impermanence and uncertainty seem to be simply what is. At least in the physical world.

"I will end this day listening to Bach's exquisite Mass in B Minor. Written to celebrate the Christian God, I will take it to celebrate all gods, for the gods of our faiths are not so different from each other. I will take it to celebrate those who believe and those who do not, for we all want to believe something. I will take it to celebrate life in its myriad forms, even as that life passes away. I will take it to celebrate meaning, even if that meaning is only the moment. The moment is now. As I gaze out the window, a slender blue heron lifts off from the shore and glides over the bay."

The Impact of a Highly Sensitive, Empathic (HSE) Nature on my Awakening

The impact is this: a spontaneous awakening of light (SAL) blows your energy field wide open! I experienced very, very intense empathic feelings for many years. Initially, I should have just been laying low, so to speak, while my energy field recovered. Instead I was experimenting with laying on of hands and picking up all kinds of emotions and symptoms from others. Mostly I felt how most people carried great sadness buried deep within. I was a novice in all things spiritual, inexperienced, and without a teacher. I just didn't know any better.

Gradually the intensity of the impact began to subside, and I learned more about my HSE nature and discernment. Identifying with the All as opposed to the ego, I absorbed and held on to emotions far less.

Nevertheless, in the beginning, HSE caused me no end of problems. Later, it became apparent that having high sensitivity with empathic gifts was a part of my nature, enhanced by my awakening, and here to stay. I began to appreciate it immensely. I found I didn't have to *express* other's emotions to know the depth of information they provided.

I learned about high sensitivity when I read Dr. Elaine Aron's, *The Highly Sensitive Person* (HSP). This was a good five years into my SAL and several years after she wrote it. It's based on the findings of her PhD research, which she has expanded upon since the book was written. She found HSP's made up approximately 20% of the population.

Her book, and similar themed books and articles written well after hers, favored the introverted sensitives a bit. Those of us who have extroverted HS natures exist; there are just fewer of us - only 30% out of the 20% HSP population. When I first read her book, I saw similarities in myself. Like most of my counterparts, though, I had incorporated the culture's bias and stereotypes of people thought to be *too* sensitive. I didn't want to be one. I told myself it was those shy, quiet types, not someone extroverted like me. Amazing how we can convince ourselves that what is staring us in the face isn't!

Western culture isn't keen on sensitive people who need down time and quiet. In the US, we're all supposed to be constant doers, "rugged individuals" taking it on the chin. This is seen as strength. As part of our culture, I looked down on highly sensitive, empathic (HSE) traits, too. For most of us, by the time we realize we have an HSE nature, we've been chastised heavily for it throughout our lives and suffer inwardly from those negative judgments. For instance, I was often called lazy by my mother. (People with high sensitivity need down-time and it gets misinterpreted.)

Divorced young with two little children, I felt envy towards those women I'd hear about in the newspapers who were lauded for being single mothers, working full-time and going back to school. I would have loved to get my master's degree at that time, but knew innately that I couldn't work *and* go back to school. Not with two kids, too. I would have been overwhelmed. I just couldn't do it (an anathema to the non-HSE natured). Nevertheless, I faulted and judged myself for this. I always felt something was wrong with me.

Then I read Dr. Kyra Mesich's book about the strong empathic nature that accompanies some with high sensitivity. She writes *all* those with high sensitivity have an empathic nature, and she suggests we see ourselves as having a highly *perceptive* nature.

This depth of empathy wasn't part of Dr. Aron's book and is often relegated to new age woo-woo. A few authors treat it as an identity (*I am* an empath) and can be fear-based, offering ways to constantly protect yourself or write whole intricate spiritual paths based on this empathic nature. The few books or articles that existed at that time weren't a fit for me.

I knew I had a strong empathic nature given my experiences, but making it who I was, my identity, while constantly guarding myself never felt right. It's not that I didn't understand what the authors were getting at.

I learned psychologically, perceptively before the SAL, that people whom I met with a lot of drama, who didn't heed anyone's advice about helping themselves were people I didn't want to befriend. This wasn't because they were "bad" or unworthy but because they kept tripping over the same rock. They didn't grow; they dumped. They offloaded their emotions onto someone else (and rarely to the person that might need to hear them).

It was about a year or so after reading Dr. Aron's book on HS that I found Dr. Mesich's book on empathy. It made sense to me and explained much. She related HS to an empathic nature and spoke about empathy extensively offering flower essences as one of the tools to help – yarrow specifically. (I also used Perelanda's ETS, in the moment, for emotional shocks; you can find them on line.)

> In her new wonderful updated guide, *The Strength of Sensitivity: Understanding Empathy for a Life of Emotional Peace & Balance*, Dr. Mesich offers the energetic definition of empathy:

"Empathic awareness is the purest form of emotional communication. Some call it the most advanced of all communication skills. It is the straight processing of emotional energy, unimpeded by intellectual filters. Neither passage of time, words, nor physical observation are required with empathic communication." She goes on to say, "Empathic communication can happen instantaneously, across any distance. It is quantum, and the experience can range from a subtle, barely discernible feeling to a profound emotional or physical symptom. ...it is a reminder that we are all connected..."

My own sense of empathic information is that the conduit for it is the *brain in the gut*; then it moves to our brain for interpretation. As mentioned before, I physically felt this process once, felt the sensed information move up from my gut and, like an ocean wave, break open on my conscious brain, informing me an earthquake was imminent. I was in San Francisco at the time and the earthquake came minutes later.

I still hadn't embraced my HSE nature fully when something I can't even remember caused the whole idea of having an HSE nature to rise up within me. As I lay across my bed mid–day, the descriptions of it came flooding into my consciousness, followed closely by highly sensitive, empathic memories from my childhood through my adult years.

You'd think I'd never read the books because it seemed a revelation. Like the descriptions of drowning people who say their whole life flashed before them in milliseconds one episode after the other, those examples of my HS and Empathic nature flashed across my psyche like a film on extreme fast forward. I teared up with recognition and finally accepted this nature as my own, grateful for the confirmation and understanding of those earlier times.

****

If you wonder if you have a highly sensitive nature, read Dr. Aron's book or go to her website.

If you sense you have an empathic nature, where you are picking up other's emotions or adding to your own, you can initially try various guarding techniques written up in books or on the internet. However, the only thing that really works in my experience is this: *not identifying with your thoughts or emotions.* Any awakening path helps you to realize that you are one with the ALL/God, i.e., the ocean rather than the drop in the ocean.

I don't say *I am* highly sensitive or *I am* an empath. I *have* those as part of my nature, but they aren't me. This can be a hard concept to get for a while; I know it was for me. (Remember what I said in the still point chapter: we participate with Life because everything is a part of God, in God, and participates as God. Even so, God is more than the sum of Its parts—Divine paradox again.)

I used Yarrow early on because I was doing a lot of clearing out of my psyche, something many of us do on a spiritual path. More and more, I came to know myself, the sustained inner calm, the whole of who I was. My empathic nature became easier for me to work with as I did this. I could recognize when I was taking something on, i.e., this emotion isn't me; I know who I am (not my emotions or thoughts). Late on my path, I began to use the following Hawaiian practice and taught it to my daughter who also has an HSE nature. Perhaps it will help you, too.

<u>Hooponoopono</u> (hoo-opono-opono):

There is a legendary story of a man known as Dr. Ihaleakala Hew Len, who healed patients in the criminally insane ward of a Hawaii State Hospital without ever seeing a single patient, unlikely as that may seem.

I read that Dr. Len set up an office within the hospital to review his patients' files without ever seeing them. While he looked at these files, he would say the words that follow this paragraph, and soon the patients all healed. He used the now legendary Hawaiian healing and cleansing method Hooponopono to accomplish all of this.

Dr. Len repeated the mantra over and over again while reviewing each file individually. After a few months, the patients were taken off medications and eventually released back into society. You can read more about this story at various sites online.

Whole paths have been created around Dr. Len and Hoopnoopono, though I never used any of them. I simply use the sentences you'll see below when I realize I've picked up someone's emotion or when I'm unclear if it's me or someone else who is feeling the emotion.

Hooponopono is based on the fact that you *are not separate from* All There Is, and as such, you accept full responsibility. When you notice an emotion, you say the following:

- **The person's name and the emotion you are sensing or just say "someone is feeling…" when you don't know its source**

   An example would be, "Someone is feeling sad." (This can include you because you may not be clear if it's you or another.)

- **I am so sorry**

   This apology is not directed toward anyone. The apology serves as an acknowledgement that we, as part of the Whole, of All There Is, are sorry for whatever has taken place to cause the adverse circumstance.

- **Please forgive me**

   We are asking for forgiveness with the absolute certainty that it has already been granted.

- **I love you (or I want the Best for You)**

   Love is a great healing power. Sending love will reverberate through your psyche and may generate an immediate feeling of well-being.

- **Thank you**

   This *thank you* is the acknowledgement that your petition has been heard and acted upon. (I often add, "Peace be with you.")

You are basically saying four things (bolded) after you acknowledge, "someone is feeling..." That's it. If it speaks to you, use it. It's the only process I know of that doesn't see the other as separate from yourself - as someone or thing to be guarded against. Dr. Mesich also provides some ideas on this in her book.

The spiritual journey is more about how you *respond* to life rather than your ego trying to manipulate or eliminate suffering out of your life. As you progress to the end of your journey, your HSE nature feels stronger. It feels this way because you see it more clearly, know who you are and so are better at discernment. It is no longer something that causes you distress; it's a trusted and useful tool. You *know* the information being transmitted without absorbing it. There are times you may still slip, but not very often.

Feeling My Way to Awakening

There was a lot of doubting over the years. My experience seemed so singular. Once I embraced my Highly Sensitive Empathic (HSE) nature, it eventually dawned on me that almost everything about my awakening was on a feeling level. It was and continues as a completely empathic feeling experience. Even with my writing, I felt it first. Yes, I'd been given a taste of other sensory perceptions -- hearing a voice, seeing a vision, etc., but my main interface with the world has been through the empathic, feeling sense. The other experiences seemed to be a way of showing me how much more there is to our spiritual biology.

My personal experience is the only way I can express to you the truth that is within all of us. When I described the SAL in "It Begins," I *felt* that Light. Being a spiritual neophyte, I had no intellectual context for my experiences. I didn't know what was happening. I knew nothing of kundalini, guru teachings, non-duality or the like. Maybe that's why intellectual understanding was bypassed or perhaps it's just my innate Highly Sensitive Empathic nature (HSE).

I *felt* something first, then later I gave it words, tried to explain it to myself in some way. I was learning concepts through my non-stop reading, and I *felt* my way to these essays that answered discrepancies for me.

Soon after the SAL, as mentioned, most everything I touched had a vibratory energy. I *felt* it. When I read other's experiences of oneness, I didn't relate. I thought perhaps I just didn't make the grade, would doubt that I was awakening, even with the SAL and its phenomena. I look back now and see that by feeling the vibratory energy within everything I touched, people included, I was *feeling the experience* of oneness. We all participate in and as this field of vibratory energy.

In the past, I had wondered about the concept of being one with everything. I'd look at a tree thinking about oneness, but there was no merging, no whatever it was that I thought I was reading about in another's experience. "Well I don't get it," I'd think. I *feel* nature, *feel* the tree, am soothed by just going outside. It didn't feel that unusual. It seems to me I've always felt the peace of nature within me. I've always felt trapped or caged if I was in the house too long. Probably a lot of people do.

I thought of other feeling experiences. I had a lucid, synesthesia dream years before I ever heard that term. There are different types of synesthesia; my dream was color synesthesia. All the colors in my dream were *felt*, not perceived in the ordinary way most of us see it. I *felt* those colors. It felt extraordinary, wonderous and new.

Also, early on, I found my body teaching me about letting go, among other things. Here's how: Kathy, the reiki healer I told you about in the introduction, was on the table so I could practice reiki on her. This was before the SAL. I was still a neophyte but could feel energy. I was intense as I concentrated on "tracing" reiki symbols in my third eye area (part of the reiki ritual and never easy for me). My hands were tense and firm on Kathy's shoulders. I was "holding on," concentrating, and my hands and wrists were hurting after a while. They didn't hurt in the ordinary way. I can't explain how it felt. The energy needed to be free from my will, though I didn't know that at the time.

Hands still in place, I told Kathy what I was experiencing. She told me I needn't hold on and concentrate so firmly or even touch the body; I could be right above it. As I lifted my hands and softened my concentration, the ache stopped and my hands took over. My body was in charge. I let my hands move wherever they wanted to go. I *felt* my way. This served me well in the year or two I was experimenting with healing, i.e., If my hands continued to want to be in a certain area on the body, I knew there was an issue there.

I noticed that for me feelings come from the gut, as in the earthquake story. Those feelings somehow move up to the brain in the head and are interpreted with words appropriate to our intellect and culture. It's knowing through the empathic feeling sense. We all probably have this sensory way of knowing to some degree.

I've learned that your experience of spirit is personal, your own. It can't be found in a book or lecture; these point the way and may be confirming, but only by looking within and honoring what you discover can love unfold.

I'm still wrapping my head around all of this. I feel ordinary. I don't mean that in a bad way; I mean I feel different from all my concepts of sages, guru's, awakened or enlightened ones. (I used the word *awakening* in my book title because you could say I awoke to *more.*) I'm not sure how to refer to myself although I've obviously changed.

Yet, this "awakening" has been my experience. I don't see the ego as evil, just something that needs to be in service to spirit. I don't talk about our physical life as a dream or illusion. It's real for what it is; but there is much more. My sense of self changed but didn't just "drop away" or "disappear." (I find these types of descriptions too airy for me; it suggests it was instant. Maybe it is for some.) Even my experience of kundalini, SAL to me, isn't as a "coiled snake at the base of the chakras."

All I know is that something transforming occurred that changed the way I see and experience the world, others and myself. In reading this book you are a witness to how that occurred, and how I overcame confusion with my writing.

And there you are. Noticing is the way, the journey in a nutshell.

You notice. You clear a lot of negativity before you realize you're OK as you are, and by the end of the process, you're back where you started but with a different perspective: a pervasive love and acceptance of self and others and each moment as it is. Sounds simple, doesn't it? It usually isn't, but join me anyway. It's worth it!

"Life shrinks or expands in proportion to one's courage."
Anais Nin

Life's Inner Journey

I spent a long time
reclaiming the parts of myself
lurking in the shadows,
not so easily seen.
I had to let go of
feeling responsible for
the happiness of others
and so many things
and embrace my Self.

It seems such a simple thing
to fully love and accept oneself,
such a simple thing, and
on the face of it, it is.
But once committed to it,
you find yourself in a labyrinth.

You see this life you
have constructed through desire,
the one you think you control
and is laid out in front of you
end over end, is really
a construct of fantasy.
And you find yourself amongst
tall hedges and the only way
through is with intuition and instinct.
You cannot see over and around
Options here and there,
one looks as good as another,
yet only one will set you free.
All your knowledge of east and west,
the direction of the sun,
the circumference of a circle,

the history of countries,
the geography of the world,
the names of flora and fauna,
all this knowledge just takes up space,
a monument to ego and will
that cannot lead the way out.

Standing dwarfed and surrounded
by those hedges, there is no clue
save your sense of direction.
And in the beginning,
familial and logical thinking can
overtake intuitive action,
and that sense of direction can lead
to dead ends, wrong turns and
long paths that seem to work for a while
but then peter out and another way
is sought and again it begins,
time after time, until finally
you plop down on the
grass below, with the sky above,
frustrated, not knowing what to do,
your eyes unable to see beyond the
labyrinth's brush, your heart distrusting
itself having kept you in this prison,
this cage, that convinced you that because
your legs were carrying you, you were really
getting somewhere. But now, you see
you are getting nowhere.
What to do; how can you cope?
You don't; so, you do nothing.
Nothing is good.
"I'll just sit here and wait."

You watch the changing sky as it shifts
like a fast-forward film montage.
You see the play of colors,

scattering clouds,
the density of fog.
You move with the wind,
and are washed with the rain,
and learn the nuances of sound –
the rustling of leaves, winging of insects, the
breath of animals as echoes of birdsong banter about.

*Everything is bound in b e a u t y
and participating in b e i n g.*

Doing nothing,
your mind drifts,
imagination dances,
and energy quickens.

After a while,
an ancient truth pervades your mind:
the meaning of life is to simply live,
and the meaning of love is to quietly give.
So, you give your Self
the gift of *Life*,
and find you are steeped in reverence.

You stand up, a bit creaky from inaction,
stretch, and find your pace is slower,
now matched with the pulse of all being.
You're no longer rushing.
You don't cry out because
you cannot see ahead.
You instinctively know which way
to go at each junction
because you listen now and *trust*,
fed by the light of the sun
and suckled by the earth beneath your feet.

You did not realize that doing nothing
would give you everything –

that the way through and out of
this maze was to give in to it,
to fall tumbling to the earth and
give way to allowing –
a parting of the waters
where transformation occurs,
where you live in each moment
knowing that when you place
value on something,
you bequeath yourself to it
and are reborn in it again and again.

You no longer worry or struggle.
You gracefully, instinctively flow
in the direction that moves you,
and, as you do, you notice
you are no longer barricaded
by the labyrinth's bewildering bushes
suggesting this direction and that.

It is not that you have come
to the end of the labyrinth. No.
It is that you no longer
define your life by it.

****

The possibilities become endless,
the moments timeless,
and being, selfless.

B. Elizabeth Atkinson
2002

The Process

Here are awakening processes as noted in Jack Kornfield's book, <u>After the Ecstasy, the Laundry</u>, a book worth reading in its entirety. The other person I'm citing is Peace Pilgrim and her diagram of process which culminates in an end to struggle. Of course, many others exist.

The main thing to know is that there are certain markers to the process that are similar in all paths. The Bliss Paper information that I intuited was my personal path and showed these same markers. If you do a lot of varied spiritual reading, you'll eventually become aware of these markers.

The *Five Stages* chapter outlined in *The Bliss Papers* is a process based on my psyche's Catholic indoctrination and verbiage. It's seems that the markers in any path are influenced significantly by the writer's culture, religious upbringing, educational training, and personal experience.

Kornfield describes two visions of awakening in more detail than I am citing here.

> *"When we compare a linear ascending path with a spiral unfolding, we find two quite different conceptions of spiritual fulfillment. The linear path holds up an idealistic vision of the perfected human, a Buddha or saint or sage. In this vision, all greed, anger, fear, greed, judgment, delusion, personal ego, and desire are uprooted forever, completely eliminated.*

> *"What is left is an absolutely unwavering, radiant, pure human being who never experiences any difficulties, an illuminated sage who follows only the Tao or God's will*

and never his or her own. If this is the ideal we hold, we also have to acknowledge that such beings are exceedingly rare or may not exist at this time on this earth.

"The more circular vision of enlightenment presents freedom as a shift of identity. In this vision, too, we awaken to our true nature, and rest in a timeless freedom of spirit. We know that our true reality is beyond body and mind. And yet because we also live within this body and mind, the ordinary patterns of life may continue.

"In the prophets of Judaism, Christianity, and Islam, and among indigenous elders worldwide, awakened beings are more complex figures who combine sanctity and flawed humanity. The difference, though, is that the old difficulties are ungrasped, held in an easy and harmless manner."

"As the sage Nisargadatta says: 'Pain and difficulty may arise, even impatience and irritation, but these have nothing to do with me. I was not born and will never die...Though this body and mind are limited according to conditions, my life is an eternal unfolding in the timeless.'"

****

Peace Pilgrim was a woman who walked thousands of miles for peace. She owned nothing and slept and ate wherever and whatever was offered to her. In the book compiled by her followers, *Peace Pilgrim, Her Life and Work in Her Own Words*, it notes:

"From 1953 until 1981 this silver-haired woman, with cheerful obedience to her calling, was a server in the world. As she approached each country hamlet or sprawling city, she carried to all she met a message of peace expressed so simply: when enough of us find inner

peace, our institutions will become more peaceful and there will be no more occasion for war.

"...Her pilgrimage for peace began on the morning of January 1, 1953. She vowed 'to remain a wanderer until mankind has learned the way of peace.' Peace Pilgrim walked alone and penniless with no organizational backing. She walked 'as a prayer' and as a chance to inspire others to pray and work for peace. She wore navy blue shirt and slacks, a short tunic with pockets all around the bottom in which she carried her only worldly possessions: a comb, a folding toothbrush, a ballpoint pen, copies of her message and her current correspondence." Her stages on the next page are scanned from her book.

Peace Pilgrim's Chart of Her Spiritual Growth

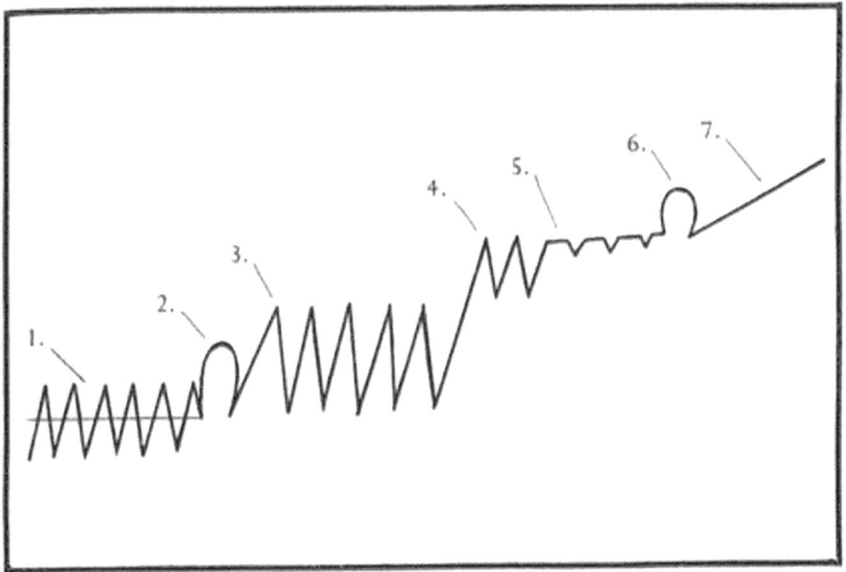

1. The ups and downs of emotion within the self-centered nature.
2. The first hump of no return: Complete willingness, without reservation, to give life to serve the higher will.
3. Battle between the God-centered nature and the self-centered nature.
4. First peak experience: A glimpse of inner peace.
5. Longer and longer plateaus of inner peace.
6. Complete inner peace.
7. Continuation of growth on a steadily upward path.

Peace Pilgrim didn't use some of the vernacular of current spirituality. In the stages above, "self-centered nature" refers to the ego. In the book and her videos, she expands on these stages. She had an experience of Light around #4. In #6 she speaks about finding peace without "slips" and being *unshakeable in all things.* She goes on to describe #7 as *an end to struggle* – meaning "resisting what is" and living in the present moment. She mentions also that these stages aren't always in this order. There is lots about her online, in written and video form, if you've never heard of her or want to know more.

<u>This is important</u>: you will *never* read or hear a spiritual process *exactly* like your own –– spiritual markers, yes; journey the same, no! Stop comparing and trust your own journey. Even as you identify with All There Is, that All works through you as an individual.

From, *The Inspired Heart – An Artist's Journey
of Transformation*
By Jerry Wennstrom

"Enlightenment is not a grand finale that leaves us blissfully risen...above the suffering of the world. It is deep and unconditional surrender to what already exists and total trust in the larger inherent intelligence which is willing to lead the way. To accomplish this is to die to everything we think is our personal identity, however intelligent, successful, and noble we think it may be."

Soul Musing

B. Elizabeth Atkinson

I am rooted in the Light; all fears are groundless. * We are all imperfect; what's important is to love ourselves in spite of it. Shadow has power when we don't. * We give time to that which we value. * When we honor the Self, we are called to do no less than honor all around us.

* The body is an instrument played by the Divine; listen to its music. Respond to it with spontaneous right action in the moment. Be the uninhibited dancer and move to the rhythm of Spirit. * Abdication of responsibility to the inner Self always creates struggle. * Self-love comes from living in a manner in which you do not betray yourself.

* Clarity is the Truth of your experience. * Do what is best for you in any given situation. Acting with love, what is best for you will invariably be beneficial to others. * We discern with whom we want to spend time: we have a kinship of Spirit with all whom we encounter, not necessarily a kinship of personality.

* We are called to respect everyone as a spiritual being, yet may not respect someone's actions as a human being. * You don't need to try and make something happen. It happens spontaneously. It rises out of its own accord, its own need to be created. And it happens in the moment, as life presents its possibilities – as what is created presents itself. This is the essence of nature.

* The only prayer is saying, "Yes!" * Allow and yield. Spirit knows your highest good and constantly supports your efforts to attain those desires; the Universe wants Itself to succeed. * Everything, every thought, every

person in your life is telling your story and supporting it. * God is so I am.

* When people's actions speak from their highest selves, everyone listens. * To choose freely is to be conscious. * The power of choice is in your ability to change your perceptions. * Comparing yourself to others is a useless endeavor. Stop comparing. It's not important what you think you can't do or be. What's important is to know who you are and to be it. * Your body is the interface between the seen and the unseen. It is God's medium. * How others behave towards me has no bearing on who I am. * In the school of life there are no prerequisites for love. * When you place value on something, you bequeath yourself to it, and are reborn in it again and again. * Become a mirror by which others can see themselves whole.

"To be born as a human, to take this particular form, is to be challenged. Even for the awakened ones, life is not always smooth. As I like to remind people, even when enlightenment comes, even when you realize the innate and natural freedom of being, it doesn't get you a pass on life. It doesn't mean you're never going to go through anything difficult. Quite the opposite. The more awake we become, often the more capable we are of having life hand us bigger and bigger situations as our capacity to accept and embody our spiritual essence grows. So life can and does respond to that growth, and in many ways it tends to demand more and more from us."

Adyashanti, Falling into Grace

Acknowledgements

This book was a long time in the making. I gratefully acknowledge the kindness and support of my children, Amber Atkinson and Justin Hibbard. Harvey Jackson has been a mainstay of support along with his encyclopedic knowledge of all things spiritual and digital. Justin put together the book's cover and website; Harvey formatted. Amber, Harvey and these friends read and commented thoughtfully on my draft: Nancy Butz, Joy Becker, Diane Williams and Christine Pillsbury.

My long-time friends Elaine Landell and Roberta Soules have been there for me through thick and thin. Kathy, Valli and Lorna bolstered me during the opening of my SAL.

Beautiful souls all, I am most grateful they are in my life along with my daughter-in-law, Brynn Albanese, and her amazing violin music, and Meg's women's circle who always listened to my musings in those early years. A big thank you to all the authors of the spiritual books that help me understand, adjust to, and embrace the SAL experience.

The truth is, there hasn't been a book, friend, family member or person with whom I've interacted that hasn't helped me progress on this amazing journey of Life. I am grateful to each of you.

About The Author

B. Elizabeth Atkinson lives amongst friends not far from the ocean in California. You can contact her at her website, theblisspapers.com, and find her poems, *Enough and Life's Inner Journey and her essay, Accepting Ourselves, on YouTube.*

What People Are Saying

"The author conveys authenticity in a creative manner. I could feel and experience how real she is as she recounts her experiences and describes the challenges, questions, and insights which have led to an awakening of wisdom that continues in her life. Elizabeth also provides guidance, poetry, and relevant experiences from others who have also journeyed on this wonderous adventure. Her book provided me with inspiration and insights for my own spiritual journey." **-Harvey Jackson, Professor of Philosophy, Howard Community College, MD**

"Kundalini, spontaneous awakening, metaphysical mysteries...If you've experienced any of these, you are not alone. Elizabeth Atkinson has been there too and shares grounded insights and reassurance for you along your spiritual path." **-Kyra Mesich, PsyD, author of The Strength of Sensitivity, www.drkyra.com**

"The wisdom is profound. Elizabeth's style is inviting, maintaining an intellectual tone, yet also appealing to the mundane in all of us. She is definitely a teacher." **Ruth Cherry, PhD, author of Living in the Flow: Practicing Vibrational Alignment; Accepting Unconditional Love; Transformation Workbook; and Open Your Heart.**

www.ingramcontent.com/pod-product-compliance
Lightning Source LLC
Chambersburg PA
CBHW031347060726
47590CB00007B/2663